PRAISE FOR *BREATHE. WRI*

"Lisa Tener's *Breathe. Write. Breathe.* beautifully explains the essential connection between mindful breathing and regular writing. All writers, and especially the millions of blocked and resistant writers, will benefit from the simple, easy-to-follow practices eloquently described in *Breathe. Write. Breathe.* Highly recommended!"

—Eric Maisel, author of dozens of creativity books, including *Unleashing the Artist Within*

"Most writers would learn astrophysics if it helped unlock the holy grail of writing flow. But Lisa Tener shows us how to consistently write with magic…in a way that's as easy as BREATHING. This is such a fresh approach to writing…and this hypnotic book is like enjoying a creative writing retreat, in usable chunks for everyday life. I'm excited about all the great writing that *Breathe. Write. Breathe.* will unleash in this world."

—Tama Kieves, USA Today featured visionary career coach and bestselling author of *Inspired & Unstoppable: Wildly Succeeding in Your Life's Work!*

"*Breathe. Write. Breathe.* touched me deeply, because it approaches writing in a whole new way. Lisa Tener focuses on digging deep into oneself, on centering oneself, and on writing from the spiritual core of one's being. Lisa provides excellent and unusual suggestions that will help you better understand yourself and your book (or writing) so you can develop your voice naturally and enhance your craft whether you are a beginner or a pro."

—Padma Venkatraman, award-winning author of *The Bridge Home* (Global Read Aloud Selection) and four other multi-award winning middle grade and YA novels

"Something truly magical happened while reading *Breathe. Write. Breathe.* One exercise, in particular, transported me on an incredible journey, revealing that I was in the midst of a deep, metaphoric process of rediscovering joy and untapped creativity."

—Renee Baribeau, author of *Winds of Spirit*

"With wit and honesty, Lisa Tener invites writers at all stages to find inspiration on the page through guided meditation, physical movement and breathwork. Grounded in research and filled with thoughtful writing prompts and exercises that promote mindfulness, *Breathe. Write. Breathe.* is both an accessible and useful resource and a playful and unique jumping off point for tapping into one's creative potential. This book will certainly breathe new life into your writing practice, and it may even help you feel more present in other aspects of your daily life."

—Julie Gerstenblatt, author of *Daughters of Nantucket*

"Not since childbirth class have I thought about breathing in so meaningful a way. Lisa Tener's *Breathe. Write. Breathe.* shares practical, engaging, and fun ways to be present—exactly where you want to be when writing. It's like having your very own breathing coach right there with you encouraging you each step of the way. Read this book, and your creative and authentic voice will soar!"

—Robin Kall, podcaster/host of Reading with Robin, event host and champion of books and their authors

"In gorgeous, dreamy prose (Tener, a book coach, knows her craft!), *Breathe. Write. Breathe.* balances warm encouragement with sound practical advice. Pick an approach or mix and match (there's plenty to choose from), but rest assured, these powerful exercises go beyond helping you grow as a writer; they help you grow as a person."

—Dr. Craig Malkin, author of *Rethinking Narcissism*

"Creativity is the great healer, and Lisa Tener's brilliant book presents potent methods for tapping into this transformative part of ourselves. Unlike other books on writing, *Breathe. Write. Breathe.* doesn't just help us hunt for the muse in our minds, but rather grounds our creativity in body experience. By integrating ancient breathwork practices from qigong and yoga with creative writing, the book shows us how to tap into our subconscious. This is where our creative powers lie waiting for expression not only on the page but in our personal growth, as well.

Finally, a book on writing that addresses the whole person—mind, body, and spirit."

—Dr. Adam Zwig, singer-songwriter and psychologist

"Lisa's wisdom, insight, and exercises were instrumental in helping me finish my book proposal and ultimately get my book published. I highly recommend *Breathe. Write. Breathe.* to any writer looking to bring more creativity and clarity to their writing process."

—Carla Naumburg, PhD, author of *How to Stop Losing Your Sh*t with Your Kids, Ready Set Breathe*, and more

"Lisa Tener's *Breathe. Write. Breathe.* is a must-read book for those who write. Through heart-felt stories and thought-provoking life observations, Lisa will open your mind to many joyful possibilities to explore with your writing. Once you experience her well-explained breathing exercises and innovative writing prompts, you will truly come to know the amazing benefits of deep breathing and understand how it is the ultimate source of power, strength, flexibility, speed, health, and vitality. Use this insightful book to learn to breathe deeply and realize your full creative writing potential."

—Lynne Heinzmann, award-winning author of *But Cats Don't Talk, Frozen Voices*, and more

"Laptop. Coffee cup. Tension. These are a writer's daily companions. No one knows this better than Lisa Tener, consummate coach and editor. In this book, she shares wise, easy, time-tested techniques to banish the companion no writer needs—tension. I'm not meditative. I don't have a place of stillness. But, hey, they worked for me."

—Jacquelyn Mitchard, author of *The Deep End of the Ocean*

"Lisa Tener's *Breathe. Write. Breathe.* is a beautifully written and engaging guide for writers seeking inspiration and practical tools for getting their creative juices flowing. Informed by her expertise as a writing coach and writer, as well as by her personal explorations of ancient and modern healing traditions, Lisa's book explores the connections between breath, mindfulness, and creativity. Not only will you learn how to connect with your inner muse, you're quite likely to enhance your overall health and well-being!"

—Patricia Muehsam, MD, pioneering physician and award-winner author of *Beyond Medicine*

"Let yourself play in these profound pages and your words will flow forward easily...as a radiant and prolific writer."

—SARK, author/artist, PlanetSARK.com

BREATHE. WRITE. BREATHE.

18 ENERGIZING PRACTICES TO SPARK YOUR WRITING AND FREE YOUR VOICE

LISA TENER

AWARD-WINNING BOOK COACH
CREATOR OF BRING YOUR BOOK TO LIFE®

PROSPERITY HOUSE MEDIA

Cover design: Tamara Monosoff

First printing June 2024

ISBN: 978-1-957565-01-9

TABLE OF CONTENTS

FOREWORD

Every time I talk with Lisa Tener, I get an infusion of energy.

We first met at a networking gathering at a mutual friend's house. I already knew of Lisa. As a writer and a coach myself, I had found her website while checking out my competition and was shocked to discover that such a highly regarded writing coach lived somewhat nearby. (We both live in the magical—and tiny—state of Rhode Island, where everything is somewhat nearby). Lisa taught on the faculty of Harvard Medical School's continuing medical education publishing course. She was an award-winning coach. Her clients' books were bestsellers. Even as I appreciated the example she set, I was intimidated by her.

At the meeting, we gathered in a circle—some of us seated on couches, others on foot stools or hard-backed chairs dragged in from the dining room—and took turns introducing ourselves. I almost fell off my ottoman when Lisa said her name.

When it was my turn to introduce myself, I swallowed hard and said that I too was a writer and a coach and that I'd recently published a book called *A Year of Daily Calm*. Had I seen Lisa smile when I said that? Or was I imagining it? Not wanting to appear too eager, I took a deep breath and turned my head to hear the person sitting to my left introduce herself, hoping it would steady my racing heart.

After our sharing was over and we mingled and partook of snacks,

Lisa came up to me and said, "It's so great to meet you. Your book sounds right up my alley! Maybe we could write a book together someday." I left that meeting walking on clouds—I'd made a friend and gotten an idea, all while having fun and socializing.

This combination of enjoyment, inspiration, and connection is Lisa's specialty. Since then, we have walked on the beach where she has shared her favorite qigong moves with me. We've attended book signings together and strolled around afterward, sharing ideas while eating ice cream. I even had her as a guest on my first podcast, *How to Be a Better Person*, where Lisa led me through the Meet Your Muse exercise that she shares in Chapter 3.

I loved creating the podcast, but felt burned out from writing and releasing five episodes a week at that time. I was lucky enough to have sponsors, but now that I was contractually obligated to deliver a certain number of listens every month, I felt I couldn't take a break. I reached out to Lisa to see if she had any advice. She had the perfect exercise, she said, and offered to talk me through it while I recorded so it could not only help me, but also be a podcast episode that helped others. (And I would have one less podcast episode to write that week!)

I closed my eyes as Lisa guided me along an imagined path to a clearing in a forest. In my mind's eye I found myself standing beside an enormous tree, with a grandmotherly gnome peeking her head out of a door located at the tree's base. She invited me into her cozy home—I miraculously made it through the tiny opening—and handed me a platter piled high with cookies. I asked this gnome how I could keep going without feeling buried in work, and she gestured to the platter of cookies as if to say that I didn't need new tips to share. I already had plenty.

I didn't know what to make of it at first, but over the next few weeks I realized I could replay old episodes and ended up airing previously released episodes for six months. My numbers stayed high, my sponsors happy, and taking time off from creating new episodes gave me space to realize I needed to shift formats and topics. (Sometimes, you are so consumed with the doing that you don't see any other options.) Now on my podcast I interview writers about how they stay connected to their creativity, which fills my well and is a lot less work. And it all started thanks to one of the exercises you'll encounter in this book.

Many listeners also reported to me that Lisa's Meet Your Muse exercise helped them find a creative solution to a vexing situation or helped them write from a more inspired place.

The time you spend with Lisa on these pages, experiencing the simple yet powerful exercises she shares, will open doors in your mind and your heart to possibilities, ideas, and energy that existed all long—they just needed an invitation to make themselves known. This book provides that opening. I can't wait to see where it leads you, and your writing, next.

Kate Hanley
Author, *How to Be a Better Person, Stress Less,* and *A Year of Daily Calm*
Host, *Finding the Throughline* podcast

INTRODUCTION

Find Your Breath and Free Yourself to Write

What does breathing have to do with writing?

The short answer: I stumbled upon a connection that forever changed my writing life.

Before: Experiences of creative flow were fleeting. I suffered through long fallow stretches of little or no writing. While I started many books, I only completed and published one over the course of two decades.

All of this changed when I incorporated simple, ancient, and time-tested movement and breathing practices into my writing routine. The words flowed consistently and with ease. My creativity flourished. I wrote from a higher state of being, if you will, and it showed. My prose grew more precise and uplifting. I had more to offer my readers and myself. I became a prolific writer.

The experience was surprising, spontaneous, and joyful. I felt exhilarated, took more risks, returned to experimenting with poetry from time to time. I had fun writing blog posts, published chapters in books on creativity, and began work on several of my own books. I published the first of those—*The Joy of Writing Journal*—and won five book awards! I read my poetry in public and learned that it touched people.

I took this discovery into my work with aspiring authors, writers, and people who wanted to improve their writing for work or creative fulfillment. Coaching clients and participants in my Get Your Writing Done and Bring Your Book to Life® programs reported a similar uplift in their writing practices:

- Those who were stuck experienced breakthroughs.
- Former procrastinators became consistent and thriving writers.
- The writing often improved, becoming more original as writers found and expressed an authentic internal voice. They took risks on the page that paid off in potent prose or poetry.
- Those who wrote for work found that their emails, reports, and other communication improved dramatically and catapulted their success in unanticipated ways.
- They accessed new levels of wisdom, insight, humor, playfulness, and beauty as writers and people.
- Writing became a delight, a joy, even an ecstatic act.

What will the practices in *Breathe. Write. Breathe.* do for you? I expect you'll find much of what my clients, students, and I have enjoyed. Perhaps more.

USE *BREATHE. WRITE. BREATHE.* TO ITS FULLEST

You can work through *Breathe. Write. Breathe.* on your own or enjoy the adventure with a friend. Alternatively, you may want to go through it the first time on your own, and engage a friend, colleague, or writing group the second time around.

BREATHE.

In each chapter in a section titled "BREATHE," you'll learn one or more generally quick breathing/movement practices designed to relax you, activate your creativity, and put you in a state of flow. Most of them come from ancient spiritual and health traditions, such as yoga, Chinese Taoist arts like qigong and tai chi, Sufism, Kabbalah, and Buddhist meditation. These traditions offer breathing and movement exercises that are easy to learn, though they may take years to master. The good news is you don't need to be a master to start benefiting creatively from your very first try.

I also draw upon practices I created and employ regularly with my coaching clients, and other exercises I learned from colleagues, mentors, and even online sources (all credited). The rich variety of options can expand your creative consciousness, and experience your writing in ever-expanding ways. While it may be easiest to try these exercises in the order presented, you are welcome to skip around and find an exercise especially fitting for your mood, challenge, or goal.

The intent is to experiment, with an open mind, and see what works for you. I invite you to discover the ways in which different practices influence your writing process. Perhaps several will enter your repertoire of creativity boosters. One day, you may feel inclined to be still and breathe deeply. Another day, you may need active movement to get your creative stream flowing.

Most practices have an associated video or audio. The link is at the end of the exercise if it's important to read the text once before practicing. Otherwise, you will find the video/audio link before the written instructions. You are welcome to scan the QR code with your cell phone to watch or listen to the recording, or type the URL into your browser to watch or listen, or just to follow the written instructions. A digital device isn't required, but it can be helpful, particularly with more involved practices, or if you want to be led through a meditation or other experience with your eyes closed.

WRITE.

After the "BREATHE." section of each chapter, you'll come to "WRITE."—with a series of writing prompts. Consider them jumping-off points. Try one or several. If you read a prompt and feel inspired to take it in a new direction, by all means do so. Let your intuition guide whether to use the prompts, or instead to return to any ongoing projects or work at hand—an essay, article, screenplay, proposal, short story, or book, for example. There's no right or wrong here. You might try a prompt one day, and dive right into your ongoing work the next time. Have fun experimenting. If a prompt feels inspiring but not right for the moment, fold a corner of the page and return to it at another time.

Please note that an ongoing project is not necessary. You may simply use these exercises to practice: writing, breathing, opening up to new creative realms, taking risks, trusting your intuition, working with symbols and metaphor, etc. In short, anything you want to practice. Allow for the possibility that your response to these exercises may generate a complete piece—flash fiction, a poem, a short story, an essay, or even a novel.

In addition, you may find that a prompt resonates with a project you have set aside. A Hay House author who participated in my weekly writing program shared that while she had no trouble writing the how-to portion of her chapters, she struggled to find compelling narratives to draw readers into each topic. The prompts provided an opening into her chapters that circumvented linear thinking, initiated creative associations with the rest of the material, and provided apt stories to engage readers in delightful and surprising ways. You, too, may find the prompts relating in some magical way with your other writing. Keep an eye out for such synchronicities and gifts!

In the back of *Breathe. Write. Breathe.* you'll find a list of all the practices in the book, so it's easy to return to a specific one you might want to revisit. "My Notes," which follows, offers a place for recording thoughts on your favorite practices: what you experienced, what you liked, and any challenges that came up.

Do you need to respond to all the prompts? Absolutely not. However, I encourage you to try them all, as you may find certain exercises help for different challenges, genres, or moods. The variety encourages experimentation and innovation—plus it's fun! And you may find many exercises to return to over time.

If a practice in *Breathe. Write. Breathe.* holds particular power for you, stick with it for a few days before moving to the next one. It's nourishing to be a writer who reads, but even more important to be one who writes. By delving into a practice for a few days, you support the habit of writing.

If you have any questions or want to share your experience, go to LisaTener.com/Breathe, or just share your comments on any blog post of mine. I promise to answer.

If you want to start with a writing prompt, but the one in a particular chapter doesn't feel right in the moment, turn to "More Writing Prompts for Adventurers" in the back of the book—you are sure to find one that inspires you—or go to the Facebook Group "Write and Create with Lisa Tener" for more. You can also ask others for their favorite practices and prompts for particular uses.

JOIN THE FACEBOOK GROUP:

Write and Create with Lisa Tener

https://www.facebook.com/groups/writeandcreatewithlisatener

Let's begin our journey together.

AUTHOR'S NOTES

- In addition to stimulating creativity, many of the practices in *Breathe. Write. Breathe.* offer great benefits to your well-being, such as relaxation, rejuvenation, increased blood and lymph flow, and more. Some of the practices in this book are more energetic than others. If you experience pain, dizziness, or other discomfort, stop the practice. If in doubt, consult your medical practitioner before practicing. Listen to your body and don't ever force a practice. You can also find ways to tailor a practice to your needs: You can imagine doing it in your mind, rather than doing it physically. Or you can do it sitting rather than standing. Be creative and mindful.
- In the first two chapters, I refer to research studies. For detailed information on these studies, see the References section at the back of the book.

CHAPTER 1

Breathe for Inspired Writing

> "When you move slower than the world, and breathe more deeply than the world, you awaken a consciousness beyond any world."
>
> —Matt Kahn, teacher, healer, author

Some funny things happened on the way to my becoming a prolific writer.

One involves a nickname I gave myself in college—"Queen of the Shallow Breath." Because, while taking an acting class, I noticed that everyone else in the class seemed to "get it." I watched their bellies round and expand followed by their solar plexuses and then their chests. I watched the progression of their breath as it filled their lungs from deep in the lobes seemingly up to their collarbones. Me? I felt like I was wearing a corset that had been laced so tightly I almost had to gasp for air. As the class focused its attention on so-called "belly breathing," I was baffled. Didn't understand it; didn't know how to do it no matter how hard I tried. And I tried hard.

I also noticed that I was absolutely the worst actor in that class. Something about the breath gave my classmates access to their creative genius. This was my introduction to the power of breathing—or, at least, to observing its power and its relationship to creative flow as it related to acting.

After graduation, the yoga and tai chi classes I took helped me become more consistently open to this state of creative flow.

Then, along came Leah Franklin, who had just returned to our hometown after five years of studying qigong—the ancient Chinese tradition that works with the mind, breath, and body movement—with a Grand Master from China. Hearing her talk about "qi"—or "life force"—I knew I wanted some of that! Maybe it could help more than my energy, too. My writing felt "off" (when I wrote at all). Could this breathing be the key to what I had missed in acting class, the secret to creative abundance?

In Leah's introductory breathing workshop, she taught us how to breathe fully into our lower abdominal pelvic floor or "dantian," loosely translated as "sea of qi" or "elixir field." Once we got the hang of breathing deeply and expanding the dantian, we were taught additional breathing techniques that helped us connect energetically with the natural world.

My long-term fatigue evaporated, and creativity took its place. I became a productive writer—as if someone had turned on the spigot for my writing to flow anytime, anywhere, with ease. And it didn't matter what form it took—blog posts, books, poems, journaling. I found that writing after qigong practice, in particular, produced consistently inspiring results. The combination of deep breathing and movement provides a calm yet energized state from which spontaneity emerges in one's writing and fresh ideas flow.

I learned to breathe deeply—"abdominal" or belly breathing became the best friend my writing has ever had, way up there with the words themselves.

Please join me in the exercises that follow to nurture your own magnificent friendship with your breath!

NATURAL STANCE

Natural Stance properly positions the body for relaxation and provides optimal benefit from many practices you will learn in this book.

Watch the video of Natural Stance and follow along, or use the script below to practice.

WATCH THE VIDEO:

Natural Stance

https://lisatener.com/natural-stance

NATURAL STANCE: THE STEPS

- Stand with your feet shoulder-width apart and parallel.
- Imagine growing roots from your feet, deep into the earth.
- Unlock, or slightly bend, your knees.
- Tuck your tailbone, as if sitting on a tall stool.
- Relax your shoulders. You may want to roll your shoulders back and down a couple of times to help them relax. Or scrunch them up as you breathe in, and release your shoulders down as you exhale with an "ah" sound.
- Tuck your chin.
- Rest the tip of your tongue on the roof of your mouth, behind your front teeth.
- Relax your jaw and gently smile.
- Relax all the muscles in your face.
- Imagine someone lengthening your neck and spine by pulling you up by the hair in the center of your crown.
- Congratulations, you are in Natural Stance!

BREATHING THROUGH WRITER'S BLOCK

If we're not aware of our bodies and our breath, we're not present. And when we're not present, it's difficult to communicate with our readers because we're not open to our full experience; we're resisting something—sensation, emotion, unease. Once we connect with our bodies through the breath, we have access to the sensory memories required for good writing. We can recall deeply how things look, feel, smell, taste, and sound; therefore, we can generate an experience for our readers. This somatic access brings our writing to life.

The other day, while working on a blog post, I got stuck. I had trouble connecting the various ideas in the post. I scanned my body and realized I'd been holding my breath and resisting sensation. Rather than breathing fully and being present, I was lost in my head.

I got up from my chair and did Qigong Bouncing—a practice you will learn in Chapter 2—to relax my body. Then I took a few gentle breaths that began deep in the belly, expanding into my solar plexus and up into my chest. I focused on the flow of my breath and nothing else.

When I returned to the blog post, I felt softened, as if the previous hard edges dissolved. The internal tension I had felt, melted. I saw clearly how to connect the ideas in my article.

Research shows that deep abdominal breathing relaxes the mind and the body. Studies also show that when the mind relaxes, creativity flourishes. Breathe deeply and you relax, allowing you to open up to the creative flow.

These two steps can make all the difference in your writing:

1. Breathe mindfully to become relaxed, aware, and present.
2. When you are present, cultivate self awareness and embodied presence to choose the scenes, dialogue, specific words, and ways of communicating that will stir—and be meaningful to—your readers.

If you are writing a memoir, this presence helps you remember minute details from your past. If writing how-to or other prescriptive nonfiction, this presence offers an intimate connection with your readers so you can anticipate their needs. For poetry or fiction, this presence expands access to infinite possibilities and potential for innovation.

As you practice the following breathing technique, you will likely experience some relaxation and subtle shifts. Over time, breathing will become more robust, more fluid, opening up new inner—and outer—worlds.

Time to breathe.

BREATHE.

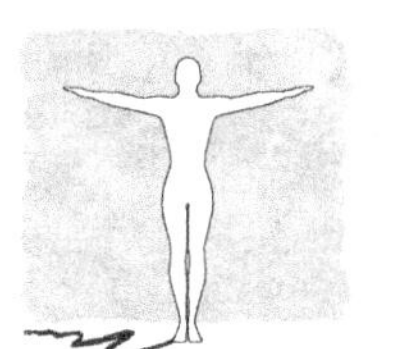

BREATH AWARENESS AND ABDOMINAL BREATHING ABDOMINAL BREATHING

It's often easiest to practice abdominal breathing while lying down, but you can do it sitting or in Natural Stance as well, especially as you become more practiced. Read the instructions. If you prefer to be led through the exercise, play the audio at the end of the exercise.

- Lie on a mat on the floor or on a bed with a pillow under your knees. A pillow under your head is fine, too.
- Place your right hand on your belly below your navel, and the left hand just below your ribs.
- Slowly breathe in through your nose focusing on the area below your right hand, as you watch your lower belly rise, then your upper belly rise.
- As you exhale through pursed lips, tighten your abdominal muscles, pulling the belly towards your spine and allowing the belly to return to its original position.
- Practice this for two or three minutes, or more.

Practice as you listen to the abdominal breathing audio:

LISTEN TO THE AUDIO:

Abdominal Breathing

https://lisatener.com/abdominal-breathing

Breathing from the belly like this turns on the parasympathetic nervous system, the part that relaxes you, helping you access your full creative range. For our purposes, in writing, this will be a powerful tool. If you want to become a ninja breather, you can continue to work on abdominal breathing at a more advanced level.

ADVANCED PRACTICE

Eventually, you'll want to experience the breath effortlessly filling your lower belly, near the perineum, below your navel, above your navel, and gently into your solar plexus and chest, as well. An even, continuous, smooth inhale and exhale. Many teachers only have you fill the belly and not the chest, but my qigong teacher emphasized the importance of the full breath that begins in the belly and expands the whole respiratory canal. Over time, you can extend your practice to five to ten minute sessions, three or more times a day.

This practice was inspired by the deep abdominal breathing I learned from Leah Franklin, my first qigong teacher, during a much more detailed and comprehensive workshop, which I recommend if you get the opportunity.

WRITE.

- **Explore Breathing:** Set a timer for ten minutes. Start out by exploring your experience with the breathing exercises, incorporating several of your senses—sight, sound, taste, touch, and smell, as well as the more ethereal, such as what you sensed or imagined:

- What did you notice about the practices?
- What challenges or memories came up?
- What thoughts or emotions arose?
- What did you dislike or enjoy most about the exercises?
- What opened up for you?

When the timer rings, you can choose to stop or keep writing. If you are working on an ongoing writing project, turn to that and write for twenty to thirty minutes, or more. See if you can keep some awareness of your breath as you write. Does your breathing become restricted? If so, observe how this affects the flow of writing. You can also put a hand on the restricted area and breathe deeply for two or three breaths before returning to the writing.

- **Turn a Trigger into a Character**
  - Write about someone who triggers you at work or in your family or friend group and how they "make you feel."
  - Now imagine how they feel inside based on the emotions they trigger within you. Write about this. Can you find compassion for them?
  - When you write about a character, whether in fiction, narrative nonfiction, or for a short anecdote, you can use the breath and intention to connect with that character or person. As you breathe, imagine you feel what they experience.
  - If you like, explore a character in a current writing project using this breathing technique.
- **Interview Your Character**

  Close your eyes and breathe deeply. If you are writing fiction or narrative, imagine a character of yours sitting across from you.

What do you want to ask them? Ask. What do they say? Write it as dialogue.

- **Deep Listening**

  Spend time with others. Go for a walk with a friend, ask them questions, and really listen. What's it like to enter someone else's world? After your walk, return to your writing. Can you listen more deeply to a character in your short story, novel, or memoir, if you are writing a narrative? You can do the same when writing anecdotes in a prescriptive book.

- **Eavesdrop**

  Write in an outdoor café or another place where you can eavesdrop. Listen to other people's conversations. You can take dictation, write about what you overhear, or just capture a stranger's energy or character. Or use what you overhear to play with a change in perspective: at the top of your page, record a phrase you overhear, and engage it as a jumping-off point for a scene, essay, article, poem, or story.

BREATHE.

Take a moment to observe your breathing. Notice any areas of constriction and place your hands, one on top of the other, over that constricted spot. Take a few mindful inhales and exhales, and see if you can expand the constricted area just by placing attention on the breath in that spot.

In each chapter of *Breathe. Write. Breathe.*, we'll end our session together with a short invitation to breathe, such as what you just experienced. You'll notice each chapter's closing breathing section serves as a kind of bookend to the first and tends to be shorter. Don't let the simplicity and brevity fool you. This second BREATHE. is important. It gives you a chance to feel gratitude for the time you set aside and the fact that you showed up for your writing practice. Even if didn't accomplish what you planned—or you're not happy with what you wrote—that gratitude plants a seed for next time you sit down to write.

In addition, ending on the breath helps you transition mindfully: rather than rushing into your next activity, take a few breaths and then move on. This mindfulness helps create space in your inner world, again encouraging your energy to continue to flow, rather than contract, and for you to be present.

CHAPTER 2

Bounce for Creative Flow

"Where qi flows, writing glows." – my inner muse

BOUNCE FOR FLOW!

We're exploring Qigong Bouncing early on in *Breathe. Write. Breathe.* because it is the key to the creative flow I've been blessed to enjoy each day.

Inspiration comes to me when I practice Qigong Bouncing.

And I practice once or twice daily.

In Qigong Bouncing, I stand with my feet shoulder width apart, parallel to each other, knees unlocked, tailbone tucked. I slightly bend my knees and rebound from the soles of my feet, heels remaining flat on the floor. My arms swing loose at my sides; my neck and shoulders relax; my whole body bounces gently; and as I do that, I calm down. I breathe naturally and with ease.

Often, Qigong Bouncing puts me in an altered state, one where ideas rush in, begging me to find a pen and paper to get it all down. And I do just that: pick up a notebook, or the book in progress, or a blog post—wherever this sudden inflow of creativity leads me.

I don't have to bounce for long; it may simply be that I'm about to work on a project and I want my body, all of me, to be in sync with the work and in a state of creative flow. I'll just bounce for a few minutes. That's all it takes. Qigong Bouncing is gentle. You don't have to be an athlete or know anything.

For me, Qigong Bouncing is the simple, daily key to constant inspiration that I share with you now.

This works for everyone, including my writing students and coaching clients. I begin our live online group writing sessions with Qigong Bouncing to cultivate a flow state before we write. The result: these individual writing students and authors express from a place of creative flow, as well. We have fun together; we sometimes just laugh at the sheer flow of the song or blog post or book chapter my students are working on.

On a day that I gather with my friends Paula and Deborah to write by the sea, we start with Qigong Bouncing. Deborah says of the practice, "It's a way to program yourself for flow. Every time you bounce, you're moving from the logical mind to the creative mind. You can see it as a reset. The more you remind your body to shift gears through bouncing, the more effective it becomes." She adds another benefit of bouncing, "It also helps me shake off any negativity or emotions I may have picked up during the day. And shaking off the old energy makes space for new energy and ideas to come in."

THE BODY BOUNCE

You may have heard that rebounding or jumping on a trampoline is beneficial to your health—it moves the lymph fluids throughout the body, supports the pelvic floor (a crucial element of deep breathing), and greatly relaxes you. Qigong Bouncing works similarly and relaxes the entire body, particularly when you do it mindfully, as we will in this exercise.

But why are we bouncing in a writing book? Because bouncing supports aliveness and creative flow. Long before trampolines were invented, for centuries Taoist monks spent extended periods of time bouncing. Qigong Bouncing to fully relax the body places the practitioner in a receptive mode where they can experience an expanded state of mind. This works for writing and any type of creating, as well. Become relaxed and receptive, and you gain entry to a higher level of awareness from which to draw your ideas, rhythm, words, syntax, and voice.

I have a few theories as to why Qigong Bouncing is so effective for writing and other creative endeavors and they may all be correct:

Theory #1: The vigorous movements stimulate blood flow through the body, including the brain. More blood in the brain means clear thinking, innovative ideas!

Theory #2: Creative blocks often relate to energy blockages in the body, what Traditional Chinese Medicine practitioners, including acupuncturists, refer to as "stagnant qi." Dynamic movement, such as Qigong Bouncing and shaking, can break stagnation and free that formerly blocked energy, which can now be harnessed for creative endeavors.

Theory #3: When the mind and body are in a focused and relaxed state, we are naturally more receptive and open to inspiration.

But let's look at the actual science.

BOUNCING FOR CREATIVE FLOW: THE RESEARCH

Exercise enhances creativity as research has proven. If we simply see Qigong Bouncing as physical movement—even though it's a lot more than that—it's easy enough to understand the link. Anything from walking to dance to sports can contribute to that flow per the research. And brain scan research, in particular, has shown that creative moments occur when the mind is at rest, when it's relaxed.

Qigong Bouncing puts the two together—exercise and relaxation. And what a magical combo it is! Add some mindful breathing and you have the *Breathe. Write. Breathe.* trifecta, enabling you to write from a place of calm and flow where you have access to the full range and potential of your writing.

RETURNING TO NATURAL STANCE

Before bouncing, we'll start in Natural Stance, which you learned in Chapter 1. I'll say just a bit more about it now that you've experienced it. In Natural Stance, we align our bodies. We do that on a physical level, so that there is no undue pressure on any part of the body, and so that our bodies become relaxed, without the habitual tension and holding we may be used to. And we do it cosmically, if you will, connecting with the energies of inspiration (referred to as Heaven Qi) and manifestation or creation (Earth Qi), both essential to the creative process. You can envision yourself as a conduit between the two—Heaven above, Earth below.

A WORD ABOUT NOURISHING Qi

Another thing before we dive in: it's helpful to understand the dual aspects of the practice. There is the active (yang, in Taoist lingo) phase of bouncing, which is physical. Equally important is the passive (yin) portion, the stillness after the activity. We call this part of the practice, "Nourish Your Qi," and we incorporate it at the end.

This stillness is integral to the practice. If you've practiced any yoga, this nourishing qi phase is similar in intent to corpse pose. In being still, we give our mind, body, and spirit time and space to integrate the practice and its benefits—physical, emotional, creative, etc. You may find that during this part of the practice you feel less attached to your thoughts, beliefs, and roles. You may experience yourself as more of a neutral witness. You become receptive. This openness especially contributes to curiosity, the flow of new perspectives, and novel ideas.

I look forward to hearing what Qigong Bouncing does for you!

THE PRACTICE

Qigong Bouncing is one of the most popular exercises in qigong because it's such an easy way to relax the whole body and release tension. I first learned it from Leah Franklin. The version I share here is similar to that taught to me by Qigong Master Robert Peng, although he adds a few more steps I have omitted for simplicity. If you wish to learn from a qigong master, you can find more about my teachers' classes in the resources section at the back of the book.

If the practice doesn't stimulate the flow effect the first time around, no worries. Give it a few chances to get you in the groove. Its effects are cumulative.

Qigong Bouncing is especially wonderful to do outdoors in bare feet if weather permits, but you can practice indoors as well. Note: If you feel tired or weak, you can stand behind a sturdy chair and hold the back of it at the top for balance.

We'll start with the Natural Stance to begin. You can read the steps and use the written instructions, or watch the video and bounce along with me. In the video, I add a few extra nuances not included in the written instructions, since they could be cumbersome to read while practicing.

BREATHE.

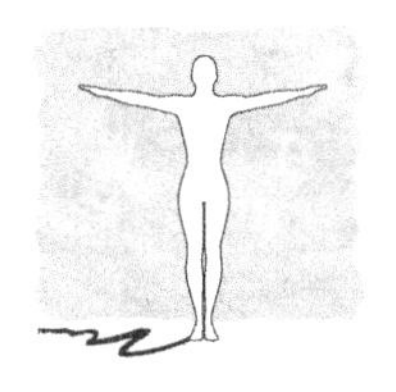

NATURAL STANCE RECAP

Begin in Natural Stance. A quick recap:

- feet shoulder width apart and parallel
- knees unlocked
- tailbone tucked
- shoulders tense up and release; relax
- chin tucked
- tongue on the roof of your mouth
- smile
- Feel as if someone is pulling the hair at the crown of your head, giving a gentle lengthening to the back of your neck.

QiGONG BOUNCING

- Bounce gently on your feet without lifting your heels from the floor or ground by bending your knees and rebounding through your feet.
- Allow your arms to hang at your sides, swinging naturally like ropes as you bounce.
- Inhale and exhale through your nose, if possible.
- After bouncing for one to two minutes or more, gently shake your arms and slowly bring your shaking arms up until they are over your head. Allow your wrists to flop above your head as you continue to bounce for another minute or so.
- Slowly bring your arms down and bounce with arms at your sides again for another minute or two.
- Come to a stop in a relaxed position, feet shoulder-width apart, jaw relaxed, shoulders relaxed, knees slightly bent.
- Inhale and notice how your body feels. Has your breath deepened?
- Notice any tingling or other sensations in your palms and allow that tingling to spread throughout your whole body.
- Place your hands on your belly, one on top of the other, and allow yourself to relax and receive the full benefit of the bouncing practice, nourishing your qi.
- Silently or aloud say to yourself, "I am in qi; qi is in me."

WATCH THE VIDEO:

Qigong Bouncing

https://lisatener.com/qigong-bouncing

WRITE.

- **What's It Like to Bounce?**

  Recall the Qigong Bouncing you just did and list 10 words you associate with the experience. Choose one or more of the words on your list and write a poem, essay, recollection, or dialogue using those words.

- **Something Bouncy**

  Think of something that bounces—a check, a ball, belly fat, a frog, a kangaroo, a pogo stick, a diving board—and write about it. Or write something from its point of view.

- **Bounce Back**

  Write about a time you bounced back—from a challenge, an activity, or an emotional state.

BREATHE.

Sitting or standing, take a moment now to witness your breath. There's no need to be an "expert" belly breather or abdominal breather here.

Relax and just practice breathing in and breathing out, preferably through your nose, naturally, easily—or as naturally and easily as you can.

As you inhale and exhale, ever so gently and softly, begin to cultivate gratitude. You can cultivate it for anything! The very fact that you wrote something today, that you showed up and read part of this book, that you're now doing this exercise, that you put pen to paper at all, that you just got up this morning and moved forward in whatever way you did—all of which is perfect, period.

Be grateful now for it, and move into even greater gratitude. Maybe it's for being alive, for those you love; but, really, here I emphasize that it's for those seemingly tiny things you would otherwise miss.

As you breathe in and breathe out, be in gratitude for your life.

That's it!

CHAPTER 3

Your Muse Is Calling

"You know instinctively what to do."

—my inner muse

MEETING THE MUSE

For almost two decades, I've led clients, workshop participants, and even doctors at Harvard Medical School's continuing medical education publishing course to connect with their creative source through a guided visualization I call "Meet Your Muse."

We use this exercise to access answers to people's writing and publishing questions of all types. Sometimes we ask the muse for a breakthrough or a shift in beliefs, such as assistance to release self-doubt and gain confidence in their writing. Or we may use it to break through some fear or self-judgment about writing.

We also use this exercise for clarity in the creative choices the writer is making—to determine the subject of a book, who the book is for, a book's structure and features, and even which idea of several is the optimal book to write. We often employ the exercise as a way to shift any thinking, habits, beliefs, and emotions that squelch creative flow. The muse provides support, specific guidance, insights, ideas, wisdom, internal shifts, breakthroughs, writing rituals, and vision.

We start by taking a few deep breaths together, releasing the concerns of the day, and settling into the present moment. Meet Your Muse is part meditation, part visualization. I usually have the writer imagine traveling a dirt path through a meadow, into deep woods, into a clearing with a small cabin, and up the stairs, through the door, inside the cabin where their muse awaits them. We've come with a list of questions, and I lead the person to ask their muse these questions, one at a time, and receive the answers.

I am awed at the creative variety we encounter. Through my clients I've met muses of all kinds—the ocean, a frog, Jesus, angels, a jester, a deceased neighbor, an ancient man, a grandma, a crone, light, a golden Buddha, an eagle. When the writer is able to let go of trying to control, answers come with ease and the writer often experiences a shift that creates space for the words to flow. This takes writers deeper into their truth, or helps them soar to new vistas.

I often envision my muse as a woman in a colorful skirt. She stands at a kitchen counter in a cabin, stirring a pot from which she serves me a bowl of alphabet soup—the perfect nurturing for a writer! Sometimes I see words form on my spoon, but often I just enjoy being nourished by letters that will form my words later.

MY MUSE SHOWS UP AS A BUDDHIST NUN

After I taught a book writing workshop in Bangkok, Thailand, I practiced my Meet Your Muse visualization, and my muse appeared as a Buddhist nun in a location reminiscent of areas I explored during the trip.

As the visualization begins, I drift into a dreamlike state and find myself in a meadow of daisies, the inner path I often walk to meet my muse. Today, though, the meadow is soon overlaid by a jungle of tall flowers, tropical ponds, and fragrant trees. My usual journey through meadow and woods becomes a ramble through this wild and aromatic garden. When I reach the clearing where I usually find my muse in a cabin, instead I find a Thai temple with ornate architecture, golden flourishes, and porcelain flowers.

I enter this temple. My muse stands before me in the garb of a Buddhist nun. She reminds me not to be so attached to anything. I sense how my wanting to control the writing and publishing process—a desire for fame and accolades—creates tension, pain, and resistance. As I lessen my grip on desires, I feel relaxed, and I experience a sense of calm throughout my body.

"Breathe," she says.

I breathe and feel my relaxation deepen.

The nun hands me a bamboo staff, taller than me, and we spar with one another. The staffs make an explosive sound as they hit against each other.

Thwack.

Wake up.

Thwack.

Stop wandering around, mistakenly thinking your thoughts about your life are reality.

Thwack.

I had come to my muse today with feelings of heaviness and overwhelm. I felt burdened by working with too many clients, which was driven by the desire to grow my business. I can serve my current number of clients, but at a cost of my creative resources. This unbalanced workload takes me away from my own writing. I ask my muse to show me where to focus my energy. I come with questions about clients, marketing, publicity, whom to hire for business support.

My muse interrupts my litany of questions and reminds me of Einstein's wisdom, that you can't solve a problem from the same level of consciousness that created it. "This is why you must practice breathing and other spiritual techniques. To wake up," she says.

My muse places a pink lotus flower in my heart. I have the sense that this is a spiritual initiation. The lotus turns to liquid gold, then violet, then spreads throughout my entire body.

I see three areas in my skull light up—the pituitary, hypothalamus, and pineal glands—the three glands associated with enlightenment. She tells me, "I am activating what you have set in motion. You have asked what to do about your resistance to writing. You know what to do. Your feelings of overwhelm oppress you because you are focusing on too many things at once. Pick one thing and be with that. Breathe."

Her touch has awakened a feeling of non-attachment to my everyday desires and preferences. My journey seems clearer. Rather than me trying to control and make things happen, my spiritual practices and writing draw me forward, like the pull of a magnet. I see my book ahead of me on the path. I don't need to walk to it. Its pull floats me toward it. I luxuriate in the ease.

I thank my muse and turn to follow the way back to my meadow. As I turn, I see white Frangipani flowers strewn across the path. I pick up one, its delicate velvety petals turning brown at the edges. I bring my nose to the sloping center and breathe in. The luscious scent enters the cavity of my skull and lights up my third eye, which tingles, activating what my muse set in motion: I am now to take a more active role in my life and work. Not active as in activity. I've done that. That's where the overwhelm originates. No, active as in discerning, choosing one focus at a time, breathing. Being in the moment, loose and relaxed, so I can easily manifest my intentions. Rather than being stressed, trying to control the outcome, and meeting my own resistance, I surrender.

I think of our sparring with the staffs and understand the wisdom of the martial artist; a relaxed body is strong, flexible, agile, powerful. A tense body is weaker, ineffective.

I am active, alert, relaxed. I choose this readiness state in my body, my qigong practice, my breathing, my thinking, my writing. Calm is a way of life that is fully alive—the deep water below the agitated surface of things.

As I walk forward, my muse calls from behind, reminding me I have the tools I need, the spiritual practices—breathing, qigong, meditation—that place me in a state of mind and being to choose intentions and actions consistent with my essence, my truth. "You know instinctively what to do."

"Wait," I turn back toward her. "What about my PR campaign? Should I cancel it? Postpone it?" I still want answers.

She tosses my staff back to me, and I catch it with ease. We spar again. This time there is a loud crashing sound. Her staff has snapped.

"You don't realize how powerful you are," she tells me. "Take an active role in your enlightenment path. Do the practices, and you will find clarity. You always wonder, 'Should I do this or that?' The practices are your foundation. Nature is your foundation. When you practice you will know. What you view as conflict, challenge, and pain, is your ally. It is there to remind you to return to the path. It is there to spur you on to practice and return to your true self."

I sense the vibration and light in my skull again. I breathe in the truth of her words, my truth.

My encounters with my muse vary—and yours will, too. Sometimes you'll get straightforward answers to your questions. Other times you can experience a huge breakthrough, new perspectives, or a radical shift in consciousness.

Many of my clients use this exercise to get clarity about their book concept and structure. For this, you can ask questions like:

- Which book (or several ideas) should I write (first)?
- Show me my readers.
- Which book idea (of several) will help further my career (or build my business)?
- What do you want me to know about tone or voice that will resonate with my readers?
- What's the best way to organize the material/book?

- What features will help my readers integrate the teaching and get the most from this book?

You can also come to your muse asking for a specific shift. A question such as, "Do I have what it takes to write this book?" can be followed by, "Help me move beyond self-doubt to embody the confidence to write this book."

We usually close with, "What else do you want me to know?"

Sometimes we see if the muse has a gift for you. If it does and the gift puzzles you, you can ask the muse to clarify what to do with the gift or what it means. Other times, you may want to offer a gift to your muse.

"HOLD EVERYTHING LIGHTLY"

Sometimes I get so caught up in planning my writing life with seriousness and forcefulness. How about you? My encounter with the Buddhist nun, reminds me to hold everything lightly—including my pen and my habits. Rigidity and control are no friends of the muse. Creativity thrives with a relaxed and easy stance, like the knees bent, feet hip-width apart position we take in qigong practice, also common to sports.

Receptivity rules with a loving, compassionate heart.

I promise myself to guard my practices with the fierceness of a mama bear guarding her cubs, but I also pledge to cultivate a sense of humor, ease, and playfulness, too, just as my muse plays with me, and the mama bear rolls around the hillside with her little ones.

Let's explore that playful attitude, as we play first with your qi ball and then meet your muse!

BREATHE.

QiGONG BOUNCING—A VARIATION

- Start in Natural Stance with your feet shoulder-width apart, imagining roots growing from the bottoms of your feet deep into the earth. Unlock your knees, tailbone tucked (as if sitting on a stool), shoulders relaxed, chin tucked, and neck lengthened (as if someone is pulling up a clump of hair at the top of your head).

- Practice the qigong bouncing we did in Chapter 2 for as short or long a time as you wish. As a playful addition, feel free to hum or laugh as you bounce. You can start with a "ha ha ha" and see if it turns into a laugh on its own. Or just smile as you bounce.
- Now, shake your hands as you bounce, first shaking hands in front of your body, then raising your hands up over your head and down toward your feet, bouncing the whole time.
- After bouncing, come to stop, in a relaxed position, knees slightly bent, shoulders relaxed, jaw relaxed.
- With your hands at your sides, notice any sensation, such as tingling, in your palms.
- Imagine that tingling feeling expanding up your arms into your shoulders, neck, head and down into your back, chest, belly, then down your legs and into your feet until your entire body tingles.
- Place your hands on your abdomen, below your navel and practice abdominal breathing (from Chapter 1), expanding your belly in all directions as you breathe in, and gently pulling the belly in toward the spine as you exhale.
- Nourish your qi by relaxing completely and saying aloud, "I am in qi; qi is in me."
- Observe your breath for 6 inhales and exhales.
- Without effort, with each breath, feel your body relax more deeply. Feel yourself become more present and connected to your body.

Qi HANDS

My muse—and your muse, too—knows how to work with energy or qi. Remember how my muse placed a pink lotus in my heart and the flower transformed into liquid light spreading throughout my body and awakening a new awareness within me? My muse has qi hands! What if you and I could play with energy the way the muse does? We can.

In this next practice, you'll awaken and cultivate awareness of your own "qi ball." This awareness of your own qi can benefit many areas of your writing life; it can help you:

- Slow down to connect more deeply with your creative source to receive inspiration.
- Focus for greater clarity.
- Cultivate a state of flow.

Watch the qi ball video and make your own qi ball:

WATCH THE VIDEO:

Qi Ball

https://lisatener.com/qi-ball

- Begin in a Natural Stance or sports readiness position, with knees slightly bent, feet shoulder-width apart. Place your hands on your belly below your navel, and continue to be aware of the expansion and contraction that comes with your breathing. Do this for 6 to 18 breaths—whatever feels comfortable.
- Rub your hands together 2 or 3 inches in front of your belly, as if you are warming your hands on a winter day. Keep your elbows bent and shoulders relaxed.
- Stop rubbing your hands, and slowly separate them on an inhale, noticing any sensations such as tingling, warmth, or a sense of fullness on the surface of your palms.
- As you continue to inhale, allow the space between your palms to expand, until your hands are about a foot apart. Can you feel as if a ball of energy is expanding between them?

- As you exhale, feel that energy consolidate or contract as your hands come closer together, without touching. You may even begin to feel a sense of resistance, as you try to bring your hands together.
- Repeat these movements consistent with the breath. Hands slowly move apart as you breathe in, and slowly move toward each other, without touching, as you breathe out. As you slow the movement and bring your hands closer on the exhale, the sense of resistance may increase, as if the energy between your palms is pushing them away from each other. Slow the movement even more as you sense the resistance. In qigong, we refer to this energy as a "qi field" and the particular field between your hands as your "qi ball." Play with your qi ball! The slower you move your hands, the more you will feel the energy of this qi ball.
- You can experiment with moving your hands far apart and close together, or making micro-movements apart and then toward each other. Observe how the qi ball feels in each scenario.
- Notice how the rest of your body feels. When you inhale, can you feel your whole body expand the way the energy between your hands expands? When you exhale, can you feel the consolidation or contraction?
- Continue to play with this qi ball. What happens when you keep your hands equidistant but slowly "spin" the qi ball so that your hands end up with one on the bottom and one on the top? Spin the qi ball slowly in different directions, and play with the expanding and contracting movements again.
- Feel the way your hands, breath, and the rest of your body synchronize, preparing you for a synchronized movement of brain to hands to pen and paper (or keyboard and screen).

This practice relaxes you and cultivates your awareness of qi. You can use it to calm your mind and relax your body to become more receptive to creative inspiration and flow.

WRITE.

EXERCISE: MEET YOUR MUSE

Read the exercise first and come up with questions for your inner muse or creative source. Then, if you like, you can use your phone to scan the QR code or go to the website link at the end of the instructions to listen to the guided meditation. If you prefer, reread the instructions to do the exercise.

- Write down one or two questions or challenges you've been grappling with. You may have specific questions about a work in progress. You can also ask your muse to confirm whether you are on track with your work. Or you may ask for more confidence. Later in the visualization exercise, we'll return to these notes to ask your muse for guidance or a shift.
- Sit in a comfortable position with your back straight and feet on the floor, or stand comfortably, feet hip-width apart, knees slightly bent.
- Close your eyes and inhale through your nose.
- Imagine yourself connecting with your source of inspiration, and cultivate a sense of gratitude for that inspiration.
- Exhale gently through your mouth as you imagine releasing anything that gets in the way of writing—self-doubt, self-defeating beliefs, fear, anxiety. Envision tension or other unwanted energy sinking down through your body and the soles of your feet, into the earth for composting.
- Breathing in through your nose, feel connected to a source of light and inspiration, imagining the light descending through the crown of your head and into your whole body.
- As you exhale slowly through your mouth, release into the earth anything in the way of that connection.
- The third time you inhale and exhale, tap into a sense of peace.

- Now imagine you are on a path in a meadow, going to meet your muse (creative source), who is waiting in the woods ahead of you.
- As you walk this path toward the woods, notice what you see, hear, feel, smell, or sense in this meadow.
- As you enter the woods, you may notice a change of temperature, a change in the quality of light, or other changes. What do you observe? What do you see, hear, feel, smell, or sense in the woods?
- You will come to a clearing in the woods where there is some kind of structure, maybe a small building or cottage. Whatever it is, you will know how to enter it, perhaps climbing the stairs and opening the door. Enter the building or structure.
- Inside, your muse will be waiting for you. Your muse may be right there at the entrance or in another room, but you know exactly where to go.
- Once you connect with your muse, note your surroundings and what you observe about your muse. Pay attention to details, as your muse may be communicating something by the surroundings, a symbolic image, or the way your muse shows up.
- Thank your muse for the inspiration it provides for your writing and other creative activities.
- Ask your first question and wait for an answer. Your inner muse may communicate through words, a felt sense (kinesthetically), and/or through images and symbols.
- If the communication feels unclear, or you don't understand a symbol, ask for clarification.
- If you don't have a specific question, ask your muse what it wants you to know about your writing right now.
- Absorb the answer from your muse.
- Continue to work through the questions for your muse. If it doesn't take you out of the meditative state, you can jot down

answers during the exercise. Otherwise, just commit the answers to memory and write them when you are done with the exercise.

- When you feel complete, thank your muse.
- Know that you can come back here at any time.
- Exit the way you came, out of the structure, into the clearing, the woods, the meadow and, when you are ready, open your eyes.

Listen to the Meet Your Muse guided visualization:

LISTEN TO THE AUDIO:

Meet Your Muse

https://lisatener.com/meet-your-muse-5

Once you complete the visualization exercise, write about your experience with your muse.

- Tell the story of your visit and what transpired.
- What did you observe in the scenery and journey to the muse? What associations do you have with what showed up on the journey?
- What did you notice about your muse? Is there a message in your muse's appearance, symbolism, or actions?
- How did your muse communicate the message and how did you experience the communication? Were there words? Symbols? A felt sense in your body?
- Explore any multiple levels of meanings, like those that may appear in dreams.
- Write about:
    - Any clarity that came about the artistic choices you are making.
    - Any shift in your beliefs or inner experience, such as self-doubt or confidence.

  - How you feel after the experience. Has anything shifted within you (beliefs, habits of thinking, ways of experiencing yourself artistically)?
- If more questions come up for your muse, feel free to close your eyes, return to your muse, and ask.
- If your muse gave you specific answers about your writing, what are your next steps in implementing your muse's advice?

BREATHE.

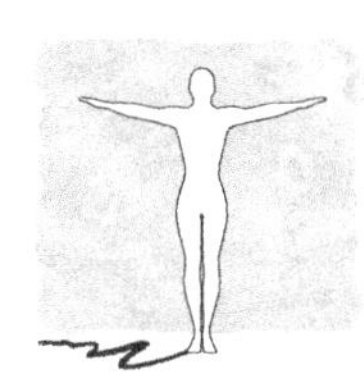

When you finish your writing practice, close your eyes and return to the connection with your muse:

- Inhale and feel that connection to your muse.
- Exhale and feel grateful, thanking your muse.

- If your muse has a gift to offer you, receive it.
- If you're unclear what to do with the gift or its purpose, ask your muse.
- Breathe and wait for clarity.
- If your muse doesn't have a gift for you, perhaps you have a gift to offer your muse.

During two decades of leading people in the Meet Your Muse exercise, I have witnessed the most glorious and varied creative genius imaginable. Enjoy the rich relationship and adventures that await you and your muse!

CHAPTER 4

The Breath of Joy

"In addition to using your mind to guide qi, use gesture and feeling to guide qi."

—Leah Franklin, qigong master instructor

Writing can stir up strong emotions. This is one reason some writers get stuck and procrastinate. This chapter offers a practice that restores joy and vitality before, during, and after writing, and provides the resources to tackle challenging material as you write.

A few weeks ago, two participants in my Bring Your Book to Life® program decided to do a virtual retreat together. They checked in with each other by phone, writing between check-ins. At one point, Leilani and Gail both experienced emotional upheaval because of the difficult nature of their subjects.

Leilani Schweitzer was writing for parents who have lost a child. While the stories in her book come primarily from parents who found peace and even meaning in their suffering, she had to traverse the territory of grief that her readers would be experiencing, as well as the pain she endured when her son died.

Dr. Gail Beck hadn't expected to find the writing distressing as she worked on her book proposal for *Dope Advice: How to Talk to Your Teens about Cannabis.* Yet, of all aspects, working on the Glossary of Terms, she felt profound sadness as she wrote about some of the dangerous combination of drugs that can be mixed with cannabis. The information reminded her of the suffering of many teens she had counseled.

Gail reached out to me Saturday afternoon for creative support to navigate the emotions and memories that arose for both of them. The three of us met on a call the next day. We began with the Qigong Bouncing you learned in Chapter 2, to get their energy moving and release any emotional pain that had built up the previous day. I also explored with Leilani how she could honor the spirit of her son. She lit a candle, which reminded her of the purpose of her writing. The book, and the connections made with other parents, is part of her son's legacy. The candle served as a gentle nudge to keep moving forward.

We then moved on to a practice in yoga called "Breath of Joy," which you'll learn in just a few minutes. Maybe you know it?

Both Leilani and Gail felt a sense of release and relief as they practiced first the bouncing/shaking and then the Breath of Joy. It helped them stay with the message of their writing without having the emotional content stop them in their tracks. They used the bouncing and Breath of Joy before writing in order to prepare, while writing when they felt overwhelmed or stuck, and at the end of their writing session as a way to transition back to their lives feeling replenished.

In addition to clearing any blockages, Qigong Bouncing and Breath of Joy can help you feel a sense of safety in writing, knowing that, no matter the emotional content, you have the tools to move the energy, to release and let go of any "stuck" energy, and to open to your inner resources. You may notice an inner shift with the exercises. You may find that you have more flexibility to explore challenging material while having a perspective that transcends tragedy, trauma, or fear.

Breath of Joy and bouncing are not just helpful for writing about difficult material. You may find that they help when you feel self-doubt, worry that no one will want to read what you write, or despair that you're not a skilled enough writer. These practices can help you enter the present moment with a renewed sense of vitality, well-being, purpose, confidence, or curiosity.

An even more surprising benefit is that these uplifting practices can affect your readers directly. Would you like your readers to experience an opening? Receptivity? Expansiveness? Joy? As Breath of Joy opens you to such qualities, they may infuse your writing with a new freedom that your readers can feel.

Perhaps you've experienced this simple yoga breath. If so, consider this an invitation to bring it to your writing routine and see what happens. You can practice anywhere. If you can, step outside on a porch, the grass, or a beach. Your bedroom or living room works, too.

BREATHE.

Experience the Breath of Joy as you follow along with the video.

WATCH THE VIDEO:

Breath of Joy

https://lisatener.com/breath-of-joy

BREATH OF JOY

- Begin by standing with your feet shoulder-width apart.
- Exhaling, bend your knees slightly and, bending at the hip, lower your arms toward the floor.
- With a deep inhale, raise your body back to an upright position, elbows slightly bent, and hands rising up in front of you at heart level, as if you're ready to conduct an orchestra.

- Rather than exhaling, take a second inhale as you open your arms out to the side, still at heart level.
- Without exhaling, inhale one more time as you raise your hands overhead.
- Exhale with a "ha" sound, bending at the hips and knees, allowing your arms to fall and sweep down, hands toward the earth or floor.
- From this slight squatting position, begin the sequence of 3 inhales and an exhale again.
- Repeat a third time or more, as long as you don't get dizzy. If you tend toward low blood pressure, go slowly and stop if you feel at all faint.
- When you come to a stop, close your eyes and see how you feel in your body. Notice any internal shifts or sensations.
- Now bring your attention to your interaction with your environment—the air on your skin, any smells, or taste sensations. Notice the sunlight on your eyelids and any color you see in your mind's eye. What sounds do you hear?
- Open your eyes; take in the sights around you.

WRITE.

You may want to start your writing practice by recording your observations during the Breath of Joy—sights, sounds, smells, textures. See if they provide an entry point or gateway for your writing, whether you plan to write a specific chapter or section of an ongoing project, a spontaneous poem, or anything in between.

Here are a few additional prompts you can choose from:

- **Smell Joy:** Is there a smell that you associate with joy, such as the scent of a particular flower or pie baking in the oven? Write about that smell and see where it takes you.

- **Imagine a Room**: Bring to mind a room in your childhood home. As you inhale, conjure up the smells of that room. What comes into your memory as you recall those smells? Write about it.
- **Joy as Poem**: Imagine the Breath of Joy as a poem. What does it want to say? Take dictation!
- **Dance Within**: Imagine what happens deep in your body as you breathe the Breath of Joy. Picture what moves inside you at a microscopic level and how it moves. Is it like a dance? What kind of dance? Do you feel something awakening within you? How would you describe that something without thinking too hard but just allowing yourself to be playful and free in your imagination?
- **Ask Joy**: Think of a challenging scene, essay, or chapter you're working on. Write or type at the top of the page, "What does joy want me to know?" Repeat the Breath of Joy. Then, write as if joy is answering the question. Allow your joy to inform your writing, even in the midst of struggle or pain.
- **Joy at Work**: Make a list of ways you can bring more joy into your work or workplace. Choose one or more, and explore.
- **Memory of Joy**: Remember an experience of joy and write about it.
- **Joy Dialogue**: Create a conversation between joy and another emotion, or between yourself and your joy. Write a dialogue and see how they/you interact. If the two emotions seem disjointed from each other, ask if another resource or emotion wants to come in as a bridge. What does it have to share? Stay playful. There's no right or wrong way to write or experience it. It may feel light or complicated or forced. No worries. You're here for the ride, so ride on.

Feel free to use these prompts on their own or as gateways to another project you're working on. Continue to breathe deeply as you write.

Allow the joy of being fully alive to permeate your writing. Imagine this life force energy in both your heart and the heart of your writing. Imagine the joy infusing your readers' experiences.

BREATHE.

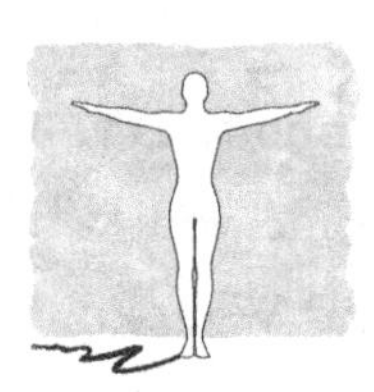

When you're done writing, inhale a breath of gratitude for this joyful practice. Exhale a sense of peace. Know that you can elevate yourself and others through this simple practice of breath, movement, and presence.

Feel free to repeat the Breath of Joy, if you like.

If the writing felt especially emotional or challenging, perhaps you want to transition to your next activity by getting outside in nature. You can go for a walk with a friend or on your own as a way to reconnect with everyday life.

CHAPTER 5

Cutting Through Procrastination

> "When you consciously decide to breathe more slowly and deeply, you alert your body to the fact that you want it to behave differently. You are not just changing your breathing pattern, you are making a full-body announcement that you are entering into a different relationship with your mind and your body."
>
> —Eric Maisel, author

Deep Writing. The title of the retreat appealed to me immediately. Five days at the Kripalu Yoga Center, with creativity coach Eric Maisel, to finally focus on my book.

Maybe even complete my first full draft.

I imagined myself rising before the sun, practicing qigong by the lake surrounded by the Berkshire Mountains. Simple foods, quiet time, and lots and lots of writing. Yoga Dance at noon—moving my body joyfully to music with others. How often do I dance anymore? Then, after lunch, more writing.

I often hear from participants in my own writing programs that the group energy helps reignite their writing practice. Maybe a group writing session could do that for me, too?

And yet, I don't sign up right away. In fact, I wait for months.

Why do I wait? First, I blame cash flow. Let's wait and see what the New Year brings. Then I have the money in hand, but I worry about missing my favorite week in my garden if the weeping cherry tree decides to bloom when I'm away.

I love to lie in the hammock, under the weeping cherry, staring up at the clouds of pink blossoms against a clear blue sky. I listen to the thrum of carpenter bees and the beating of hummingbird wings. Some years, the weeping cherry blooms just as the forsythia reach their height. The yellow splash, the cascade of pink, the blue sky. Perfection. This is my absolute favorite time in my yard. I won't miss it.

A week before the workshop, I beg the cherry tree to bloom. I wait. The forsythia buds, pokes out, then seems to burst into its full golden glory overnight. Will the weeping cherry follow?

Easter comes—the first day of the workshop—and I still haven't registered. The forsythia leaves unfurl their green prayer flags as the yellow blossoms fade. The cherry buds appear ready to bloom any day. I want to see its majesty, but it's dawning on me how badly I crave this writing retreat—for the writing, for the book, for progress, for support. Why do I need, or think I need, outside support to write? I don't know, though I feel certain it will help.

I call Kripalu and discover that, yes, there is still room in the workshop. Still, I waver throughout the day.

When I finally decide to go—two and a half hours before the workshop begins—I feel inexorably propelled. I can't not go! I call to reserve my spot. The desk has just closed. Do I drive the three hours in hopes they will admit me? In hopes I can get a room?

I must. All that waiting, all that wavering, and now I feel sure.

Three hours later, here I am, at the retreat. For five days, I align with my passion. I write during class. I write at night. I write in the wee hours while it's still dark out.

I write everything I've outlined and think I'm done. And then I write more—stories I'd forgotten I had in me, new writing prompts for my readers, a breathing practice I learn at Kripalu. The flow astounds me.

What are the secret ingredients that contribute to the flow?

- The beautiful, safe space that Eric Maisel creates for us, a container within which to write and write and write.
- My qigong practice every morning, once I discover a private yoga room where I can stare up the mountainside as I connect with the qi of earth, heaven, and my own body.
- The beauty of the woods, lake, mountains, early spring wildflowers and, above all, the weeping cherry trees which remind me of my own tree blooming back home.
- Being in a room with a dozen or so others just writing for hours on end. In short, community.
- No distractions. Just the page, the pen, the writing.
- Having my outline from which to write. And then writing beyond what I outlined—turning to my daily experiences, qigong practice, and nature for inspiration.

Making this list reminds me that I can bring similar insights into my writing life at home and work.

DEVELOPING YOUR WRITING PRACTICE

Are you, too, waiting for the stars to align to start writing? Yes, my Kripalu retreat served as a catalyst to complete most of a first draft of my book. Yet, in Eric Maisel's Deep Writing workshop I learned what it takes to write daily, no matter where I am. I established a practice and continued with it when I returned home. I also remembered a practice I'd developed earlier and returned to it—that of visiting my "Inner Garden," an interior space from which writing flows with ease.

As modern writers, we may find our minds flitting from one duty or worry to another. What will I eat for lunch today? What might go wrong at work tomorrow? What should I have said in that argument with my mother? How do I get my son off his video game?

This type of thinking doesn't serve us, yet it can take up a remarkably large part of our mind space. When writing, such thinking can sabotage you before you even start. Such worry energy often leads to procrastination and keeps us from the certainty that propels us to write consistently.

One simple way to bypass this worried, planning, distracting inner voice is to gently shift your focus. Create an inner world where writing and flow is your norm. Today's breathing and writing exercises will help you do just that.

WELCOME TO YOUR INNER GARDEN

We're about to visit your Inner Garden, a place where you can leave that sabotaging perspective behind and plunge yourself into a nourishing environment that supports mind, body, spirit, and creative pursuits!

We'll visit your Inner Garden two ways. For now, read the text and imagine your Inner Garden as best you can. Later in this chapter, you'll find a QR code to an audio recording so you can be guided through the meditation/visualization.

- Lying down or sitting up with your hand on your belly, deeply inhale as your belly expands both in front and to the sides and back of your body.
- Feel your belly release and relax as you exhale.
- Close your eyes.
- Imagine a verdant, walled garden in front of you.
- While you can't see above the tall walls, at the gate you can peek through the slats and see a hint of the beauty that awaits you.

- The garden seems to go on and on—a vast landscape.
- Perhaps you glimpse a waterfall in the distance or a bed of pink roses. Maybe you even get a whiff of their heady scent as the breeze blows it your way.
- Know, with every nerve in your body, that when you open this gate and enter the garden, you are on sacred ground. Take off your shoes.
- Before you step in, leave your baggage outside the gate. Let go of that suitcase of judgments, blame, and shame you've been dragging around. Just leave it here.
- That wallet with your ID card? All IDs must be left as well. Let go of who you think you are on a day-to-day basis.
- Allow your writing practice to teach you who you are beyond your limited ideas, habits, thoughts, and beliefs.
- If you're wearing a down parka, by all means, take it off. The garden is warm. Shed any layers you want before you enter.
- Feeling lighter? Good.
- Breathe deeply as another whiff of roses or jasmine or lilacs floats your way. Open the gate and enter the garden. This is your inner landscape, and you get to design and discover the rich, varied terrain over time.
- Walk around inside this infinite Inner Garden and find an inviting spot to sit down and write.
- Know this inner space-time as the gift it is, outside of everyday time and space, where the laws of physics no longer hold. Gravity-shmavity—you can fly.
- Over time you will explore many aspects of this inner landscape, or maybe you'll sit in the same spot all the time. It's your cosmic reality.

Here are some things I've noticed about the inner landscape: There is a freedom here. Freedom from worries, from daily responsibilities, from the limitations of the smaller you that you may think you are. In that freedom you discover the more expansive you—new states of consciousness, new ways of being and experiencing life. There is no room here for judgment.

YOUR GARDEN REFUGE

Just by entering the gate and closing it behind you, you signal to your mind that this is not ordinary time. This is something magical, mysterious, mystical. As you deliver that liberating message to your mind, you gain access to the magic, the mystery, and your inner mystic.

The weeping cherry is a portal for me, existing in my actual garden and in the inner landscape I visit sometimes when I write. You can connect with your own Inner Garden as a place of refuge and calm where the outer world falls away and inspiration flows.

BREATHE.

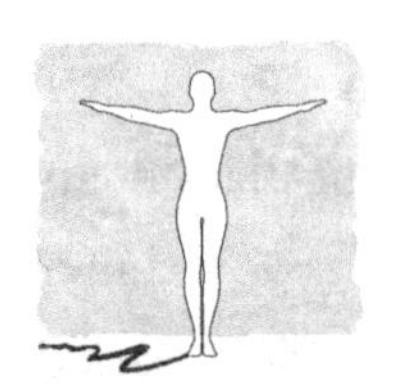

BECOME A FOUNTAIN OF CREATIVE ENERGY

What's a garden without a water feature? I grew up in Rego Park, Queens, in New York City, with a postage stamp of a garden behind our house, where my dad built a little waterfall and pond about the size of our kitchen sink. He framed the pond with a few dozen gray rocks, using the larger ones to create a foot-high wall for the water to cascade down.

The waterfall was my favorite part of the garden, even more than our swing set. It felt magical, squeezed between two small hemlocks that seemed like titans to pre-school me. Sometimes that diminutive waterfall appears in my Inner Garden.

You may enjoy many varieties of water features in your Inner Garden—ponds, waterfalls, rivers, streams, ocean, tide pools, brooks, hot springs. How about becoming a water feature, though? Today's breathing exercise comes from the qigong practice called "Fountain." Think of the continuous flow of a fountain, the gush of water and negatively charged ions which shower you—and all surrounding life—with a sense of well-being and even euphoria.

In the Fountain practice, you embody flowing water. In many ancient systems, such as qigong and yoga, the water element is associated with creativity and flow. The flow of qi in Fountain supports the kidney and bladder meridians (energy pathways in the body). Also associated with creativity and the water element, kidneys are seen as a reservoir for vitality. Thus, the flow generated when you practice Fountain can energize you, enhance creativity, and cultivate joy and well-being, which all feed your writing.

As we get into the Fountain posture for optimal flow, I'd like to point out an important energy center. As you stand, feet hip-width apart, you may notice a place on the sole of your foot, just above the arch, where you feel enhanced sensation. In Chinese traditional medicine and martial arts, this spot is called "Bubbling Springs," indicating that the energy of the earth bubbles up through this point and feeds our kidneys, where life force energy is stored. In practicing qigong, we can imagine Bubbling Springs drinking the vitality offered by earth as we inhale, releasing any stagnant qi on the exhale.

You may want to take a moment to explore this simple connection among earth, Bubbling Springs on the soles of your feet, and the breath as it travels through your legs and into your belly and kidneys and back down into the earth. You can read the instructions or watch the video to practice Fountain.

WATCH THE VIDEO:

Fountain

https://lisatener.com/fountain

FOUNTAIN

- Close your eyes and stand on the floor (or mat or earth) with your feet shoulder-width apart in Natural Stance.
- Unlock your knees and tuck your tailbone, as if you are sitting on a tall stool.
- Lift and tense your shoulders on an inhale.
- Release your shoulders down and relax on an exhale.
- Tuck your chin.
- Place your tongue on the roof of your mouth.
- Smile and relax your body.
- Placing your hand on your belly, take a few deep inhales and exhales, allowing your hand to rise and fall against your abdomen along with the rising and falling of the breath.
- Notice that the breath expands throughout your body—in front, to the sides, and toward your back, not just in front.
- After a few deep breaths, focus your attention on the Bubbling Springs energy center in the part of the sole of your foot just above the arch.
- As you inhale, imagine your body drawing nourishing earth energy up through Bubbling Springs in your feet, up through the inner (facing) parts of your legs (this is the "kidney meridian") and into your belly.
- As you exhale, the stale qi returns to the earth for rejuvenation. (Think composting.)
- Inhaling, bring fresh qi up through Bubbling Springs into your body.
- Exhaling, release.
- With your arms at your sides and the backs of your hands facing each other, inhale as you bring the backs of the hands toward the center line of your body, about an inch apart, and let your hips and buttocks slide back slightly.

- As you tuck the tailbone under your body (and move your spine in a wavelike motion), raise your hands, back to back, up to the height of your shoulders.
- Exhaling, open the hands to face away from you, wrists bent, and then out to the sides, as if your hands are a fountain of water flowing up and out. Allow your hands to gently drop as the fountain of qi falls around you. Qigong teacher Lee Holden describes this action as "a wave rolling up through the spine and out through the arms."
- Repeat this flowing movement 6 or 9 times, cultivating what Lee calls "flow in your body, relaxation in your mind."
- To bring the flow to a close, at the end of the last exhale, bring your hands in front of your belly, facing each other. Take a couple of deep breaths in and out through your nose, and then turn the hands to the earth in thanks.
- Place your hands on your abdomen, one over the other, and nourish your qi by taking a few relaxed breaths into your lower dantian.

"As writers, we are our own instruments."

—Dani Shapiro, author

WRITE.

- **Enter the Gate: Your Practice Time**

I invite you now to use the Inner Garden visualization from earlier in this chapter to open today's writing practice. You can use this QR code for the audio recording to guide you, or go to the website for the recording. I also include the text below the QR code if you prefer to read it. After the meditation, answer the Questions for Reflection.

Listen to the audio to Explore Your Inner Garden:

LISTEN TO THE MEDITATION:

Explore Your Inner Garden

https://www.lisatener.com/explore-your-inner-garden-2

- Close your eyes and imagine yourself at the gate to your Inner Garden.
- Consciously think about what you would leave at the gate and imagine putting that "baggage" down at the entrance to the garden.
- Imagine walking through the gate and entering the garden.
- Explore:
  - What time of day does it seem to be?
  - Where is the sun in the sky?
  - What season is it?
  - Do you see any paths? If so, choose one and walk it, observing what you notice.
  - What plants grow here?
  - What animals do you see or sense?
  - What water sources do you discover—rivers, ponds, waterfalls, fountains? Is there a cave with an underground spring? Do you come upon an ocean?
- Find a space in your Inner Garden that feels conducive to writing, and settle in. Perhaps find a spot to sit on the ground. Notice the feel of the earth in this spot. What do you see around you?
- Breathe into your lower belly, feeling your breath expand all the way down to your perineum with each inhale.
- Allow the breath to gently expand from deep in your belly up into your solar plexus and chest.

- Ask yourself:
    - Do you notice any scents in your garden?
    - What do you hear?
    - What are the qualities of the air—crisp, heavy, moist, warm, or cold?
- When you have explored the space, imagine getting comfortable in it.
- When you feel ready to write, open your eyes.

QUESTIONS FOR REFLECTION

- Write about the inner journey. What did you observe or sense? Explore:
    - What happened?
    - Did this practice open up anything for you, and if so, what?
    - What did you discover about your voice?
    - Will you try this practice again? Why or why not?
- Pick one phrase you wrote that you love and write it here or in your writing journal:

  ____

- Continue writing. You can use this opening practice to continue work on an ongoing project, or to inspire a short story, blog post, essay, poem, or other experiment.

BREATHE.

When your writing practice feels complete, close your eyes and take a deep breath, perhaps imagining a particular scent or image from your Inner Garden. Is there something you wish to leave here in your garden? Or anything you wish to take back with you to remind you of this sacred space? If you want to envision returning with something from the garden, such as a flower, imagine asking permission before you pick it.

Know you can return to this Inner Garden at any time. When you do, you may feel drawn to the same spot, or you may be called to a new spot. Allow your intuition to guide you.

If you feel so moved, return to the practice of standing and opening to the earth's energy through the Bubbling Springs points in your feet. You may also return to Fountain and feel the beautiful flow as your body gets back into movement after sitting and writing. Does Fountain feel different in any way from when you practiced before your writing session?

CHAPTER 6

Like a Whirling Dervish

"You are the universe in ecstatic motion."

—Rumi, thirteenth-century Sufi poet and mystic

I stand on the beach, arms outstretched, bare feet in the sand, and slowly spin counterclockwise. Ocean. River. Sand dunes. Beach. Ocean. River. Sand dunes. Beach. Ocean-river-sand dunes-beach-ocean-river-sand dunes.

Beachoceanriversanddunesbeachoceanriversanddunesbeach. As my spinning speeds up, the scene becomes an indiscernible blur of blue and sunlight and green and sand. My breath unconsciously deepens.

I whirl in place, and then my body darts out like a top, spinning along the shore toward the river. I'm grateful to have Narragansett Beach almost to myself at this early hour before the throngs have arrived by motorboat, car, and jet ski. The morning is mine, and I fill the space with my joyful dance.

I know in every cell of my being why the whirling dervishes spin. Soon I smile and feel the kind of ecstasy that one aspires to in a spiritual practice. It easily rises from nothing, whisking up the particles that form my cells and organs, my thoughts and beliefs. For a short time I am remade of stardust and the clear glowing goo of jellyfish plasma.

When I come to a stop and hold my hands to my heart, my insides continue spinning until they catch up with the fact that my external body has ceased movement. Slowly, the particles of my being come together, arranging themselves anew.

After whirling, creative inspiration flows, and I take out my journal to make notes and write poetry.

Did you ever spin as a kid—arms stretched wide, turning, turning in circles? Watching the trees and houses around you become one great blur? You pick up momentum as the joy rises within you, faster, faster, until you plunge to the ground, dizzy. You giggle with a friend, a brother, a sister, or a chirping bird.

I first learned the practice of Sufi Spinning as a fairly new mom, and it immediately lifted my sleep-deprived exhaustion and provided a sense of renewal. I had quit work to stay home with my baby, and moved with my husband to a neighboring state where I knew only a handful of people. I joined my local MOMS Club and found that other exhausted new moms yearned for something to rejuvenate themselves as well.

We pooled our resources to hire a babysitter for our toddlers while a dance teacher led us in all kinds of world dance—from hip hop to belly dancing to African and jazz. When our teacher introduced us to spinning in the style of the ancient Sufi mystics, the world fell away and my heart opened like a spring bud.

This dance of the Sufi mystic still has the power to lift any mood I find myself in and infuse me with joy in a minute or so. I cannot help but smile and maybe laugh. Some of my best creative work comes from this joyful state. When I begin my writing practice with Sufi Spinning, I often find myself penning ecstatic poetry or other work that transports me to a new understanding of life and its meaning.

Jalal al-Din Muhammad Rumi developed Sufi Spinning (or Whirling) as a form of prayer or meditation in the thirteenth century. And he created approximately thirty thousand verses of poetry! Rumi's works continue to be translated the world over. I cannot imagine it to be an accident that one of the most inspiring and inspired poets of all time was the first whirling dervish. If you want to elevate your consciousness and write exquisite poetry, or just experience a whole new level of inspiration, give this practice a—ahem—spin!

This simple movement may become a favorite of yours, as well.

BREATHE.

SUFI SPINNING PRACTICE

A note before we begin: This physical practice may not be for everyone. If you have ankle or knee problems, balance issues, or creaky hips, perhaps you can practice in your mind's eye, rather than physically. If this is the case, close your eyes and picture yourself out in nature, somewhere beautiful, spinning around in circles. If you're feeling playful and in shape, please join me in the physical spin.

Trust your body. Do you need to keep the movement slow, mindful of your body's needs? Or does it feel best to speed up so the world becomes a blur and you become a vortex of pleasure?

If you can bring this exercise outdoors, do it. However, make sure the ground is flat and there are no rocks or stones to trip over. I love to do this on the beach early in the morning or in the evening when hardly anyone is around. While not essential, you can find Middle Eastern music on Spotify or YouTube and play it, if you like. If you're indoors, give yourself enough room to easily stretch your arms in all directions, with some wiggle room besides.

- Cross your arms over your chest, hands on your chest near your heart, and bow.
- With your hands still crossed on your chest, slowly begin turning counterclockwise.

- After a few spins, uncross your arms as you bring your hands toward your heart.
- Caress your face with the backs of your hands and allow your hands to gently rise until they are above your head.
- Spread your arms like wings, and turn your right palm to face skyward and your left palm facing down toward the earth. The right hand is slightly higher than the left.
- Keep your eyes open, gently unfocused, and build up momentum to spin a bit faster, as long as it feels safe to you.
- Be mindful not to twist your ankles or knees. Speed does seem to contribute to the elevated state of mind, but not if it injures your body. Stay mindful as you spin.
- Smile. Feel how uplifted you become as you spin.
- Feel your heart opening.
- You may naturally breathe deeply in this state. If not, consciously deepen your breath.
- Spin until you feel compelled to stop. If you can, slowly spin to a stop, crossing your arms and putting your hands on your chest, eyes closed, as you allow your inner ears to reach equilibrium and the dizziness to abate. If you feel especially dizzy, you may want to sit or even lie down, looking up.
- Pause and feel the effects of spinning.

Watch the Sufi Spinning video and follow the instructions.

WATCH THE VIDEO:

Sufi Spinning

https://lisatener.com/sufi-spinning

SUFI SPINNING, MODIFIED SITTING VERSION

You may modify this practice by sitting and visualizing.

- Sit comfortably with your spine straight and close your eyes.
- Imagine yourself spinning counterclockwise, hands crossed on your chest. If you wish, you can actually cross your hands on your chest while you imagine the practice.
- Smile.
- Imagine allowing your hands to uncross and unfurl as you slowly reach above your head and the right hand unfurls palm up, left palm faces down.
- Imagine spinning slowly at first, then gathering speed and momentum.
- Gather up the joy-promoting negative ions as you spin (in your imagination) counterclockwise.
- Feel your heart opening.
- Feel the re-orienting power of the centripetal force upon your very particles.
- Bathe in the absolute ecstasy of your inner journey.
- Then imagine stopping. Stillness. A re-orienting of self, born anew.
- Pause and observe how your body, mind, and spirit feel after imagining spinning.

If you prefer to try this seated and visualize, listen to the audio.

LISTEN TO THE AUDIO:

Sufi Spinning Visualization

https://lisatener.com/sufi-spinning-visualization

WRITE.

When you feel ready to write, hit the page—or the screen—spinning rather than running. Grab your notebook or electronic device, and make notes about the experience. If you're working on an ongoing project, feel free to go right into that, rather than taking notes about the experience. Otherwise, choose a writing prompt from the options below (or create your own inspired prompt):

- **Time Warp**: Imagine spinning and winding up in a different place and time. Where are you and when? Describe the surrounding landscape and the situation you find yourself in. Take it anywhere you want. This can become a poem, short story, sketch, or the seed of a novel.
- **Becoming**: Imagine you are spinning and, when you stop, you become another creature entirely. How does this creature experience the world—noises, smells, tastes, senses? What sounds do you make? How do you get around in the world? What do you experience?
- **Heart Space**: As you breathe, imagine a light in the center of your heart, starting as a spark. Breathe into that spark and imagine it filling with light on the inhale and expanding with each exhale. As your light grows, what does it reveal in your heart? Don't overthink this; in fact, don't think at all. Just take a relaxed and open attitude to whatever shows up. Allow it to feel playful. Don't worry about meaning or analysis here. Just play and write about the experience.
- **A Shift in Perspective**: Walk a path through the woods or a field, or walk along a city street. Every once in a while, turn around and look at the same things from a new perspective. Write about the experience. Then read something you've written previously and ask if there are other interesting ways to look at it. For example,

write from a different character's point of view, perhaps even an animal's.

If you like, allow the prompts to ease you into other writing projects. When you're done, see how your elevated state may have worked its way into your words. Was it easier to write? Did new insights come? Did it affect your voice?

BREATHE.

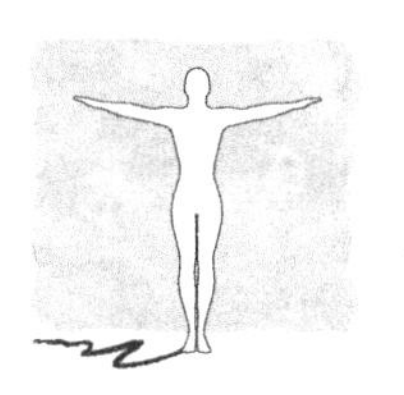

Place your hands on your heart, close your eyes, and breathe deeply. What do you notice? Think of the many whirling dervishes spinning through the centuries. Imagine the exotic Middle Eastern locales where they whirled. Feel into their presence and the power of a practice passed down from spiritual masters. Feel a sense of gratitude for the many teachers who shared these traditions, making them available to us today.

CHAPTER 7

Balancing Breath

"Lost in our minds we lose touch with our bodies and the glow that could be feeling presence goes primarily numb."

—Will Johnson, author

THE SURPRISE OF PRANAYAMA

My first visit to Kripalu Yoga Center was an R&R retreat with my future husband, Tom. Our first morning there, we got up at six and padded down the hall in opposite directions to the shared bathroom of our respective genders. In my mind, I grumbled to be getting up so early. My worn-out body needed more sleep. Should I have stayed in bed?

Thirty minutes later, however, I found myself in meditation class, practicing Alternate Nostril Breath, holding closed one nostril at a time while inhaling through the other nostril, then closing that nostril and exhaling through the other. The other times I'd practiced this breath, I found it awkward, my stuffy nose making breathing difficult. However, the yoga and healthy food had opened up my nasal passages, and I found an easy rhythm. My fears and judgments melted away, and I completed the exercise feeling a sense of calm, equanimity, and strength.

After breakfast, I wrote in my journal for the first time in months.

In fact, I wrote all weekend when I wasn't practicing yoga or walking in the woods with Tom. Life could swirl in chaos around me, but this simple breathing practice brought me into my center. Together, the breathing and journaling practices brought me into an elevated state.

In Sanskrit, the language of the ancient yogis, breath work is called "pranayama." According to the Oxford Dictionary, pranayama is "the regulation of the breath through certain techniques and exercises." The word comes from "prana" or "breath" and "ayama" or "restraint."

Yoga practitioners use the breath in many ways—to cleanse the body, to energize, and to balance body, mind, and spirit. You may wonder how this supports your writing practice. The calming quality of breath helps settle your psyche. Your chaotic, chimerical thoughts become focused and integrated. Rather than a controlling or pushing mental energy, you will find your mind becomes clearer, more supple, and open. This receptivity welcomes inspiration and makes it easier to enter a creative flow state.

According to the Chopra Center website, in addition to calm and focus, Alternate Nostril Breathing restores balance between the left and right hemispheres of the brain and clears energetic channels.

PARTAKE OF SPIRIT

Literature may romanticize writers who steep their stories—or poems—in a lowball glass, a cocktail—or three or five—for the muse. These writers' personal stories don't often end well—gun, rope, gas, or just a tortured life. AA, if they're lucky.

In my experience, simple spiritual and meditative practices, such as Alternate Nostril Breath and others in *Breathe. Write. Breathe.*, are stronger than any concoction made from alcoholic spirits.

Imbibe of the spirit, rather than spirits, and the muse will provide loving inspiration and, at times, joy beyond measure.

BREATHE.

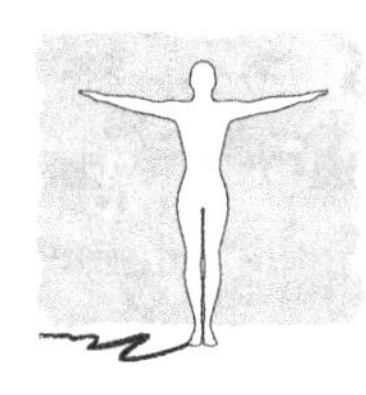

LET'S TRY ALTERNATE NOSTRIL BREATH.

Alternate Nostril Breath is a calming, balancing breath, especially as we practice it here. There are many variations with longer exhales, equal inhales and exhales, and holding the breath. Over time, you can experiment and see which one works best for you.

You can read the instructions to follow along or listen to the recording to be guided step by step.

LISTEN TO THE AUDIO:

Alternate Nostril Breath

https://lisatener.com/alternate-nostril-breath

EXPAND THE BREATH

- Let's begin in a seated position on a chair or seated on the floor, legs crossed, if that is comfortable for you. Feel free to sit on a pillow or place pillows under your knees for support. If using a chair, find one that feels comfortable and allows you to sit up straight. Use a pillow for your back, if needed.
- Note: If your nose is stuffy, later in this chapter I offer several options that help.
- Notice how you feel—thoughts, emotions, and sensations in your body. Do you experience an overall sense of relaxation, restlessness, or excitement? Do you feel discomfort in any particular areas? We will come back to a body scan at the end and see if anything has changed.
- Before we introduce the Alternate Nostril Breath, we embrace the deep diaphragmatic breath that gently fills lower belly, solar plexus,

and chest. Place one hand on your solar plexus and breathe into that area. As you breathe in, let a comfortable inhale move your hand as your solar plexus slowly expands. As you exhale, your solar plexus sinks in and your hand with it. After several breaths, breathe into the sides and back of your solar plexus, expanding its volume. Allow your ribcage and chest to expand with each inhale, as well. Do not force the breath, just gently deepen it.

- When that feels complete, move your hand to cover your navel. Breathe similarly here, at first allowing your breath to meet your hand. Then feel the whole band of mid-belly, sides, and back expanding with the inhale and releasing with the exhale. Breathe in through your nose, and out through your nose or mouth. Bring a gentleness to this breath.
- Now allow the breath to start at the navel, and expand into the solar plexus and chest in one smooth, relaxed motion, without forcing.
- Lastly, place your hand on your lower belly, an inch or so below your navel. Practice a similar deep inhale and exhale here for several breaths deep in your pelvis and then allow that to expand to your navel, solar plexus, and chest with ease.
- Scan your body again and feel free to make some notes about what you observe.

ALTERNATE NOSTRIL BREATH

- Now that we have brought the breath deep, we can start this new practice of the Alternate Nostril Breath. We'll use a simple mudra (or finger positioning). If you have learned this breath with a more complex mudra, feel free to use that position instead.
- Place your left hand face up on your left thigh, bringing the tips of your thumb and index finger together, while laying the other three fingers out flat.
- Take your right hand, and fold down the pinky, ring, and middle

fingers to touch your palm, so that only your index finger and thumb stick out.

- First, we'll practice the finger movement. Cover your right nostril with the pad of your thumb. Then release your right nostril and cover your left nostril with the pad of your index finger. Got it?
- Inhale through your nose.
- Sigh as you exhale through your mouth.
- Now press the side of your right nostril with the pad of the thumb of your right hand, closing off the airflow from that nostril.
- Inhale into your left nostril for 6 or 8 counts. Pause a moment.
- Now release the right nostril and press the left nostril closed with the pad of your index finger, closing off air flow to your left nostril.
- Exhale through the right nostril for the same count of 6 or 8. Pause a moment.
- Now inhale through the right nostril. Pause.
- Release the index finger from the left nostril while covering the right with the thumb and exhale through the left nostril. Pause.
- Repeat the full pattern of inhale left, exhale right, inhale right, exhale left 6 or 9 times, pausing briefly between each inhale and exhale.
- Pause and relax. Notice how you feel in your body.
- Continue for another 6 or 9 rounds of breathing if you wish.
- Again pause and observe.
- For a common variation, you can hold your breath for 6 counts between exhales and inhales.

Integrating the left and right hemispheres of the brain, as this practice does, supports any creative endeavor, and especially writing, where both left brain (writing, language, logic, reasoning) and right brain (creativity, imagination, art, intuition, emotions) play essential roles.

CLEARING YOUR NOSE

Did you find this practice impossible due to a stuffy nose? For a long time, I did. There are a few things you can do to clear your nose:

- Try cutting out dairy for a few days. For me, that change was magical. I rarely suffer from a stuffy nose or seasonal allergies anymore, except after a party where the cheese and crackers become too tempting, or I've indulged in a cranberry pecan loaf (who can stop at just one slice?).
- Notice what other foods may affect you; bread, wheat, sugar, and nuts are some of the more common culprits. While it may at first seem anathema to cut out favorite foods, experiment. You may discover, as I did, that dietary change can increase your vitality, optimize your health, elevate your mood, and free up more creative energy. If not, you can always go back to those foods or indulge on special occasions.
- In my early thirties I studied Polarity Therapy, a system of health and wellbeing developed in the 1970s by Austrian Osteopath and Naturopath Dr. Randolph Stone. Stone traveled throughout Asia, studying healing practices from Chinese Traditional Medicine and Indian Ayurvedic Medicine. He combined much of what he learned in Asia with his knowledge of Osteopathy, Gestalt Therapy, and other healing traditions and named this holistic modality "Polarity Therapy." In our training, we experimented with exercises from the book *Energy Exercises* by John Chitty and Mary Louise Muller. One simple practice became my favorite. By chance, I found that it cleared my stuffy nostril(s). In a nutshell, here is the remedy:

MODIFIED COOK'S HOOKUP

You can find a number of variations to this online. I first learned it this way.

- Lying down or sitting up, cross your arms over your chest and place your palms under your armpits.
- Relax your shoulders.
- Your thumbs should stick out and up and your fingers should point toward your back.
- Notice which forearm is on top. Cross the opposite ankle over your other ankle.
- Stay in this position, and breathe naturally through the nose or mouth, eyes open or closed until you feel a shift. Within a few minutes you will likely notice your stuffy nostrils clearing.
- If you don't like sticking your hands under your armpits, I inadvertently discovered you can wrap one hand around your wrist, then cross the ankles. If the grabbing hand is your left hand, cross your right ankle over the left, and vice versa.
- When this first part feels complete, uncross your ankles and leave some space between your legs.
- Place your hands in a prayer-like position in front of your heart, where the hands only touch at the fingertips and palms do not touch.

WRITE.

Sit in silence for a few minutes, and note any changes in your thoughts, emotions, or physical sensations. What is the quality of the overall energy? Write down your observations.

Now write some more. You may pick any of the following exercises, using them as a jumping-off point, or just start right in with an ongoing project.

- **Body Talk**: Choose an organ in your body—eye, nose, mouth, liver, stomach, lungs—and let that organ tell a story. Perhaps your right foot wants to tell describe a hike in the woods. Or your nose can share a walk in your garden. Maybe your liver has a tale to tell. What organ calls to you? Allow it to speak. Feel free to start with one organ and move to another. Allow your mind to remain in an open, relaxed state, without judging whether the writing is good or bad, or the exercise is complicated or stupid. Be open to whatever comes. Remain curious.

- **The Journey of a Breath:** Write about the journey of one breath. See where it takes you, both inside and outside your body.
- **Breathe Like Your Character**: Envision a fictional or true life character in a narrative you're writing—whether novel, memoir, self-help anecdote, or brief story within a blog post or essay. Imagine how that person breathes, and describe that person in an activity, paying special attention to their respiration. Allow yourself to explore the labored inhale of an elderly man lying in a sick bed, the exhilarated breath of a hiker in the forest, the shallow breathing of someone detached from their emotions, or something else.
- **Crossing Over**: Imagine any kind of journey of crossing over—from one place to another and back—just as your breath crossed over left to right and back again during Alternate Nostril Breath. Write it.
- **Transported by Scent**: Go outdoors and take in the scent of a flower. Where does the scent transport you? A memory? A place? An inner celestial space?

BREATHE.

When the writing feels complete, close your eyes and notice your breath. Do both nostrils feel fully open? Is there balance or evenness to your breathing? What qualities do you observe in your respiration? You may wish to return to the Alternate Nostril Breath, or just inhale deeply into your abdomen, solar plexus, and chest, letting your entire torso expand in all directions, then release and contract on the exhale.

Now, with eyes still closed, move your eyeballs as if gazing downwards. See where your attention is drawn within your body. What do you experience? What impressions do you get? See if you can go deeper and get to the essence of any sensations within. If your mind becomes active, just notice and release thoughts, returning again to a metaphysical look inside your body.

CHAPTER 8

Breath of Gratitude

"I will give thanks unto the Lord with my whole heart."

—Psalm 9:1

It helps to begin your writing practice renewed, recharged. If you come to your practice depleted, what do you have to give? And from where?

Start here then. Fill your tank.

What's your baseline? Do you begin with "I'm not good enough," "My well is dry," "Can't write worth beans"? If so, there's a hack, an easy way to shift your focus to gratitude.

RELAXING INTO GRATITUDE

Join me again at my Kripalu writing retreat, after a flurry of writing, late into the night. I look around the room the next morning and see my fellow writers tapping away on their keyboards. I feel grateful for the time I've set aside for my book and the community around me. A simple gratitude practice comes to mind. I tap into my gratitude for my surroundings, starting with the floor:

- How it supports me
- How the smooth, blond wood reflects the window light

- The natural designs and gradation of the wood
- The perfect design of the planks

I move to the next thing my eyes rest upon, the windows:

- How they let in light
- The view of the pines they offer
- How I see only the seven or eight boughs framed by the window and appreciate how they move in the wind

I move on to the shelving for yoga supplies:

- Such efficient use of space, tucked away at the back of the room
- Perfectly designed for its purpose
- The cheerful, light wood

Do I feel more grateful? More energized? A higher vibe? Not yet. Maybe I need to keep going. The overhead fans make me aware of air, sustainer of life. I imagine the oxygen in my lungs, in my blood, in my cells.

The judgmental voice tells me my writing stinks. I persist despite the voice, grateful for the ceiling, the way it absorbs sound, the whiteness of it, the way it keeps the floor above from falling down on us!

The clock—a reminder of this time I've gifted myself, the time given me on earth, all the experiences I've had and the remaining hours of this retreat.

The voice, "Why waste it writing junk?"

"Thank you very much, voice. I don't need your sass. I feel grateful for the time to write. The practice is the thing."

More gratitude: For ants rushing across the floor with such speed. That our earth is still healthy enough for ants to survive and thrive.

I'm struck by how tired I feel. Is this creative resistance? Insulin resistance? Something else?

TAPPING THE MUSE FOR GRATITUDE AND UNDERSTANDING

What does my creative muse have to say? I take myself through the Meet Your Muse exercise (Chapter 3), and imagine walking a path through a meadow and deep into the woods. My muse greets me in the cabin in a clearing where she often awaits my visits. Lines of ants, like spokes on a wheel, travel into her cottage from all directions. They travel up the stairs, up the stone walls of the cottage, across the roof, back down the opposite wall. Busy, busy, busy, the worker ants move constantly, move everywhere. Soon they cover every inch, overtaking the cottage inside and out. They're all over us, my muse and me, layers of ants. Their dark mass obscures everything.

The ants remind me of the busyness of my life. So many activities, thoughts, directions. I've lost sight of my inner sanctum under all those ants.

My muse tells me, "Acknowledge the ants. Acknowledge your discomfort. Be still with the ants." The ants are like that hard-worker aspect of me. I'm diligent, productive. I accomplish things. I rarely make time to truly slow down. The past winter, even my walks seemed rushed as I hurried to get in out of the cold.

Now, I sit and watch the ants as they follow each other up and around the sides and roof of the cottage. In stillness, I recognize that one thought, one ant, can change the dynamic, the flow. One simple thought, broadcast with an open heart, can lead them all away. And just like that, the dark cloud of ants disperses.

When they leave, the cottage feels cleansed, almost sparkling. I sense a clarity, as if the cottage is somehow different at a subatomic level, transformed by the ants.

The heaviness of that harsh voice is gone. I feel uplifted and restored. A deep sense of gratitude has replaced the criticism. I believe in myself, in the creative magic of my muse and its ability to transmute creative blocks in playful, unpredictable, delightful ways.

BREATHE.

KABBALISTIC BREATHING PRACTICE

Thanks to Stephen E. Hodes, MD, for permission to share this practice, which I learned from his former website, and to Rabbi Stern for teaching him.

As Dr. Hodes says about this practice, "It is simple, as all breathing exercises are, but profound. It involves focusing one's awareness-concentration on the simple exchange of the breath, in and out of the nostrils. It does not involve forcing any type of breathing or any particular rate of breathing. But usually when we pay attention to breathing, it slows down."

You can read the instructions or let the audio recording guide you.

LISTEN TO THE MEDITATION:

Kabbalistic Breathing

https://lisatener.com/kabbalistic-breathing

- Sit comfortably.
- Bring your attention to the breath at the tip of your nostrils and observe the breath coming into your nose.
- Observe the breath coming out your nostrils on the exhale.
- Notice your belly rise on the inhale and fall on the exhale, with the majority of your attention still focused at the nostrils and the air coming in and out.
- After observing for several breaths, begin to visualize "Ein Sof"—a Hebrew term meaning "God in the form of infinite, pure essence." Or imagine the Universe, infinite Spirit, or whatever term describes this infinite, pure, divine spark to you.

- Visualize "Ein Sof" directing the air into your nose and body on the inhale.
- On the exhale, surrender yourself to God (or Spirit or the Universe) "as an act of relaxation and serenity."
- Feel deep gratitude for each breath, thanking God (or Spirit or the Universe) for the gift of breath, the gift of life.

Dr. Hodes writes, "We contemplate the time between breaths as the eternal moment—timeless in its essence. We understand that the Universe exists from moment to moment as an act of continuous creation by a Will greater than our own and we accept this truth."

WRITE.

Today's prompts all work with gratitude.

- **Writing in Gratitude:** Let's continue cultivating gratitude and incorporating it into our writing, raising the quality of our energy and our connection to our creative muse.
    - Close your eyes and inhale, feeling a sense of gratitude for the air you breathe and your amazing body that turns air into energy.
    - Exhale a sense of well-being and peace.
    - In, gratitude; out, well-being and peace.
    - And again.
    - Now open your eyes and cultivate a sense of gratitude for the first thing your eyes rest upon.
    - Write about this object and your gratitude for it, continuing to tap into vibrant gratefulness.
    - When it feels complete, turn to the next thing and cultivate gratitude for it.

  - Write about all the aspects of it you observe—feeling grateful for each one.
  - Repeat this a number of times, enough to feel your mood lighten or to feel a sense of expansiveness. If you feel resistance, that's okay, too. Just notice it.
  - You can also think about a writing project and feel grateful for each aspect of it—the chapters written, the characters of a novel or lessons of a memoir, creative exercises in a self-help book, the people whose stories make your business book come to life. Give yourself time to feel individual gratitude for each element, one at a time.

Now pick something on your list and write a poem or story about it. Or just use the exercise as a warm up and delve into an ongoing writing project. You can also choose to work with one or more of these writing prompts:

- **Character Transformation**: Choose a character in an ongoing project or create a new character that could use a lesson in gratitude. Start with their initial sense of lack, jealousy, scarcity, or fear. Write about and explore an event that teaches them about gratitude or somehow transforms their experience of life from one of bitterness or scarcity to one of gratitude.
- **Your Gratitude Lesson**: Write about an experience or person that taught you about gratitude.
- **Exploring, from Lack to Gratitude**: Explore experiences around lack, scarcity, abundance, resentment, or gratitude.
- **Gratitude at Work**: If you are feeling unhappy at work in any way, explore those aspects and experiences about work which you enjoy and feel grateful for. How can you increase those positive experiences?

- **Write a Thank You Letter**: You can write to a person who's alive or someone you never met (an author, perhaps). Or write to someone you wish you had thanked when you had the chance. Or write to a younger version of yourself in gratitude for a courageous step you took, perhaps. You don't have to send the letter, but if the person is around, feel free to do so, even if you have to use the internet to find them.

BREATHE.

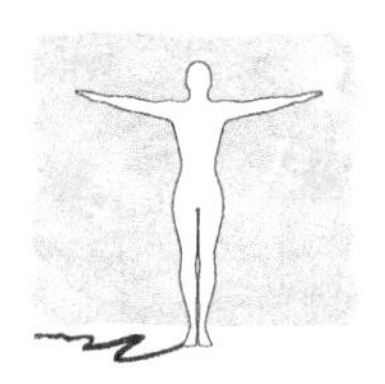

The more gratitude you cultivate for your writing practice—even when things don't go as expected—the more you nurture your relationship with your muse. Accessing creative flow then becomes easier and easier.

When you come to the end of your writing practice, return to the Kabbalistic Breathing Practice for a few breaths.

Then focus on one thing about your writing practice that you feel grateful about. Then another. And another. It may be a word you wrote, a feeling you had as you wrote, the fact that you spent time writing. It may be the pen, the computer, the chair, the sun that comes into the room and warms you. Continue to find something else to feel grateful for with each breath.

When judging, criticizing, or feeling that our writing falls short—"too little," "not good enough,"—we abuse the muse! Turning attention to appreciate any aspect of our practice, generates positive energy toward and within our muse. This feeds our relationship with our own creativity.

Whatever gratitude you feel at the end of a writing practice sets you up for connection, inspiration, and flow for tomorrow or the next day—and the next.

When you feel complete, send your creative muse one more simple breath of gratitude.

CHAPTER 9

Tiffany's Healthy Dance

"Just start dancing and the band will find you."

—Tama Kieves, author and life coach

Having been brought up without much religion, which my dad thought more divisive than uniting, it took me a long time to become comfortable in places of worship. In my twenties, while living in Boston, I eventually discovered a spiritual community that inspired me.

When I moved to Rhode Island with my husband and baby, I searched for a new spiritual home. For a short time, Newport housed a Unity Church, which met in the building of another church. Influenced by the Transcendentalist movement and by Ralph Waldo Emerson, Mary Baker Eddy (founder of Christian Science), and other world religions, the Unity spiritual movement was started by Charles and Myrtle Fillmore in the 1800s. After discovering a few friends attended this church, I decided to give it a try. I loved the uplifting music, meditations, and prayers that focused on accepting the thing prayed for as already existing (such as health, peace, well-being). The prayers are beautiful affirmations of our indwelling divinity. When Tiffany Masters, a medical intuitive from Texas, visited, offering healing sessions in the minister's home, I decided to give this a try as well.

While waiting for my session, I found myself amidst a display of dazzling necklaces—rose quartz beads, amethyst crystals of many sizes, ropes of watermelon tourmaline. Each piece of jewelry offered a poetic intention. Not just fluorite for clarity or amethyst for healing but, for example, "Moving into What Is Possible," a necklace of jade cubes and silver balls. The attached tag read, "Here to show you that when you Move deeper into What Is Possible instead of what you already have done over and over with no good result, that WHAT IS POSSIBLE is the key for you."

Tiffany, the intuitive healer who created the jewelry, later told me that she intuits the energy of each necklace and then writes up what the necklace embodies—love, clarity, healing, or financial abundance, for instance, to support the wearer in the desired outcome.

Soon after I arrived, Tiffany opened the door to a cozy healing room, followed by her black and white Pomeranian, Joshua the Super Dog. Joshua came unadorned. Tiffany wore strands of crystals that accentuated her powerful, sunny energy and gave her an air of majesty. A former executive assistant at a global communications firm, Tiffany seemed a combination of new-age healer, powerhouse, and hometown girl, with a Texas accent.

At the close of my session, Tiffany taught me the "Healthy Dance," a practice I have used for over a dozen years. You'll experience the practice firsthand in a moment, but for now, I'll describe it briefly. In its original form, you state your intention as "I am healthy. I am strong." Then clap four times.

As you state the intention, you raise one hand and, as if you are grabbing the healthy qi from above, you grab the air and make a fist, bringing that hand down toward your torso. Then you repeat the action with your other hand. The movements are synchronized with the words.

The Healthy Dance is quite easy, and you can employ it for more than healing. Think of it as a multi-tool Swiss Army knife for transformation and inspiration, a perfect way to prepare for writing from an elevated state. If you are looking for a simple ritual to begin your writing sessions with intention, vitality, and a spirit of fun, the Healthy Dance may well become your go-to practice. It combines both movement and affirmation. Here's how I began to use it for writing and creative pursuits.

HAPPY, HEALTHY BIRTHDAY, TRACY!

On my writer friend Tracy's birthday, I gave her a small blank paper journal with an iridescent textured cover and homemade card, and taught her the Healthy Dance.

After lunch, in a parking lot behind the West Bay Gourmet, where no one could see us, we moved our hips, reached above our heads as if grabbing qi and sang, "I am healthy. I am strong." *Clap. Clap. Clap. Clap.* Tracy loved it, and we shared it with our women's group a few days later. What started as "I am healthy. I am strong," soon morphed into all manner of affirmation:

"I am loving. I am kind."

Clap. Clap. Clap. Clap.

"I am wealthy. I am grateful."

Clap. Clap. Clap. Clap.

"I am peaceful. I am calm."

Clap. Clap. Clap. Clap.

Tracy and I often got together to write, and we soon incorporated the Healthy Dance in our writing practice. While the original mantra ran four beats and three beats, we sometimes squeezed in a few extra syllables.

"I am creative. I am in flow."

"I am writing. I am happy."

"I am writing. I am wise."

"I am writing. I am playful."

This exercise can help bring out aspects of your writing voice that you wish to strengthen or explore, such as humor, depth, emotion, texture, creativity, quirkiness, wisdom, etc.

Ready to dance? First, I'll teach you the original Healthy Dance that Tiffany taught me. After, we'll get creative and expand its use.

BREATHE.

THE HEALTHY DANCE

Watch the video or use the directions below to do the Healthy Dance.

WATCH THE VIDEO:

The Healthy Dance

https://www.lisatener.com/healthy-dance

- Close your eyes and notice how you feel in your body.
- Breathe into your belly and relax.
- Now open your eyes.
- Stand with your feet hip-width apart, preparing to chant "I am healthy. I am strong."
- While saying the first part of the first sentence, "I am," raise your right arm and reach toward the heavens with an open hand, as if grasping the heavenly air.
- After grabbing the qi in a loose fist, bring that arm down to waist level, elbow bent.
- Now reach with your left arm and hand as you grasp the heavenly qi in your left hand, make a loose fist, and chant, "healthy."

- Repeat the motion, chanting, "I am," as you grab qi in your right hand, and "strong," as you grab with your left.
- With both forearms and hands at waist level, clap your hands four times.
- Return to the chant, repeating the hand motion, followed by another four rhythmic claps. Really put your body into this. Move your hips and make it a dance.
- Repeat this mantra and movement as many times as you like, reveling in the playfulness of the exercise. When you feel complete, close your eyes, observing your breath and body. What do you notice? Feel free to write about the experience.

On one level, this spirited exercise naturally causes you to breathe more deeply, move your body, smile or laugh, and feel playful. Research shows that deep breathing, movement, and smiling contribute to good health. In addition, turning our attention to positive thoughts can increase happiness. These thoughts can replace the unconscious negative self-talk we often find in our heads. On a deeper level, Tiffany points out that by saying, "I am," you make a powerful decree for your intention—such as health and strength—from your own higher consciousness, what Tiffany calls your "Mighty I Am Presence." For a deeper understanding of how this works, you can check out Tiffany's website (tiffanymastersinternational.com).

When you practice the Healthy Dance throughout your day, over time you will likely discover a shift toward greater vitality and well-being. One wonderful aspect of the Healthy Dance is that it's so easy to teach others. During our first session, Tiffany encouraged me to teach the Healthy Dance to my husband and young son, and I did. When my son woke up feeling tired or sick, we often did the Healthy Dance together.

"Every day brings a chance for you to draw in a breath,
kick off your shoes, and dance."

—Oprah Winfrey

WRITE.

- **The Writing Dance**: What qualities do you want to incorporate into your writing practice today? Can you work them into your eight beat (or so) affirmation or decree? If you're going for humor, "I am funny." If you want to support your readers through a hard time, "I am nurturing." If you're looking for flow and inspiration, "I am creative." Some possibilities to get you started:
  "I am writing. I write in flow." *Clap. Clap. Clap. Clap.*
  "I am happy. I am inspired." *Clap. Clap. Clap. Clap.*
  "I am playful. I am creative." *Clap. Clap. Clap. Clap.*
  "I am clear. I am wise." *Clap. Clap. Clap. Clap.*
  Try it now with whatever words express your current intention and fit the beat. Do the dance and mantra. Remember to clap! Then write that phrase at the top of the page to see if it will bring anything new to the work. Then, write. You can use this phrase to start a new piece or work on a project in process.

If you prefer to work from a writing prompt, try one of these:

- **Heavenly Path**: While standing, start with one of the breathing exercises you've learned so far, such as the simple Breath Awareness and Abdominal Breathing you learned in Chapter 1 or Fountain from Chapter 5. Take several breaths. Reach your arms up to the heavens and, on the exhale, imagine sending a single breath to journey upwards. Where does it go? Imagine the breath as it travels into the heavens. Does the breath transform in any way as it travels? Does it stay in the heavens or return to you? Write about it. Explore.
- **Before the Workday**: Before you start work in the morning, try the Healthy Dance and bring in the qualities you would like to bring to your work. Put the affirmations down in writing, as well.

At the end of the day, journal about any effects this had on your workday.

- **I Am You**: In a café, in a longish line at the supermarket, or on the subway, notice a person and try to match their breathing pattern. Imagine what it's like to be this person, then write about it.
- **Ode to a Teacher**: Write about a teacher and a profound lesson that teacher taught you. Be expansive in the idea of a teacher—a person, an event, an illness, an injury, an animal, a plant. Teachers can be anyone or anything.
- **Affirmation Station**: Make a list of affirmations to manifest. Pick one and explore what it would feel like if that affirmation resonated and came true. What might it take for that to happen?

BREATHE.

When you complete your writing practice, close your eyes, place your hands on your lower dantian, three fingers' width below your navel, and take a few deep breaths. Notice the rise and fall of your belly, diaphragm, and chest as your breath. What do you observe? Read over what you wrote and see how the qualities you invoked may have manifested in the writing.

Close with another deep breath, hands at your heart.

CHAPTER 10

Earth Breath and the Groundhog

"Your book is alive in you."

—the groundhog you will meet in this chapter

By now you know how I love to visit my creative muse by imagining myself on a path in a meadow, heading into the woods, then into a clearing, then into her little cabin. Sometimes I don't quite make it to the cabin; other times I meet a different guide or travel an unusual path.

On one such sojourn to my muse, I breathe deeply and find myself gazing inside the greenish yellow, pollen-filled center of a daisy. The daisy becomes my portal to the same meadow where I often begin my muse journey. As I enter I see daisies, sunflowers, and sunchokes, the sunflowers' leggy cousins. I place my hands in the dirt and feel the richness of the earth. Bright sun warms my face, reminding me that we humans serve as a conduit for the earthly and the heavenly ways of being, a common theme in qigong.

My fingers touch the roots of the flowers. A groundhog digs in the soil next to me, tunneling, inviting me to follow. It enlarges the width of the tunnel, so I can fit. We travel deep and far underground, and emerge inside my muse's cabin, popping up from the earthen floor in a library, a room I have not seen before.

The groundhog smiles, showing me beaver-like buck teeth, opens its jaws further, and nabs a book with its mouth. Munch. Munch. Munch. I copy and munch a book as well. I experience the message that this is part of the process: We digest the book. We poop some of it out. The rest becomes energy, becomes part of our bodies, our cells. The groundhog communicates, "Your book is alive in you."

While I have received a similar message before from my muse, this one feels even more directive. It seems to say, "Feel the book alive inside you. Feel the book within your cells." The groundhog's message helps me locate the book within myself.

I note how the steps suggested by the groundhog inspire a new way to think about book writing:

- Dig into the rich soil before you begin writing.
- Tunnel through your unconscious.
- Ingest.
- Digest.
- Let the book become a part of you.
- Let go of what doesn't fit—perhaps the pooping out I described earlier is merely part of the editing process!
- Allow the book to come from deep within, from your very cells. Know the book as part of you and draw from those places within you where it resides.

I recall a similar message I have received before, to *be* the book, which seems meditative, spiritual. The groundhog's message seems more practical and specific, teaching me the kind of alchemy the writer engages in. It feels both magical and mundane, and isn't writing both those things?

These two aspects of the message support each other—the watery, dreamlike feeling of being the book (which I experienced in an earlier visit to my muse) and the earthy, grounded process of digging, tunneling, ingesting, digesting. These two elements can be related to the body's first two energy centers or "chakras" (according to the system of yoga): the root center, located at the base of the spine, represented by the earth element, and connected to physically manifesting; and the sacral center, located below the navel, represented by the water element and connected to the dreamy, symbol-rich state of creativity.

THE ALCHEMY OF WRITING

We write for many reasons:

- to know ourselves
- to communicate with colleagues
- to change within
- to convince
- to connect with others
- to heal
- to teach
- to change minds and hearts
- to ignite a spark in someone
- to make activists of our fellow humans
- to succeed at work
- to transform how we show up in the world
- to change the world

Feel free to add to this list!

In all our writing, whether a 200-page book or a three-line haiku, there is an alchemy possible when we allow our hearts and minds to open to those things we deeply know. You may write stories and truths you have shared before in other forms, or share what you know—and these are important. Yet, all of a sudden, even more powerful, your writing will take you into new territory—fresh words, vivid images, unfamiliar language. Your writing can take a surprising turn, tunnel underground, carry you to the mountaintop, or even leave you at the edge of a cliff.

The alchemy is this astonishing mixture of what you knew you knew, what you didn't know you knew, and what you have just realized. The alchemy rests also in the words that come to you, the unexpected image that catches your breath. Working with the elements of water and earth help us access this alchemical ability in a powerful way.

BREATHE

EARTH BREATH, EARTH Qi

Earth Breath relates to the first chakra, located at the tailbone and pelvic floor. Earth provides a strong foundation for life. Earth chakra energy feels grounded or rooted. Earth is about feeling safe. Earth energy (and the earth breath) nourishes, supports, and sustains you and your life. The earth element is also about bringing something into the world, taking it from inspiration and idea, turning it into words and then a book, for example.

Earth Breath helps us realign to feel grounded, connected to earth and home. Safe.

A NOTE ABOUT TECHNIQUES

I learned the five elemental breaths, several of which you will learn in *Breathe. Write. Breathe.*, as part of my Polarity Therapy training, a modality that healed me from chronic fatigue/fibromyalgia years ago, prompting me to study it in depth. The elemental breaths derive from Indian yogic practices and also appear in other traditions, so you may find the same name, such as Fire Breath, for several different types of breathing techniques and hand positions (mudras). So don't let it confuse you if you see a breath here that has the name of a different technique you learned elsewhere. It's kind of like the name Sophie, which belongs to my dog and also to my niece. Two species, one name. No problem.

You can read the instructions or let the video guide you.

WATCH THE VIDEO:

Drawing in Earth Qi

https://lisatener.com/drawing-in-earth-qi

DRAWING IN EARTH Qi

We'll break this into two parts. First, we'll breathe the Earth Breath and connect with the qualities of earth. Then I'll share a way to draw earth energy up into your body.

EARTH BREATH

- Sit in a comfortable position or stand in Natural Stance. For the purpose of the video, I will stand.
- Remember that breathing from deep in your belly, as well as your diaphragm and chest, brings the greatest benefit to your whole body.
- Place both hands on your belly, three fingers' width below the navel, one hand on top of the other.
- As you inhale through your nose, allow the breath to expand your lower belly, pressing against your hands, and gently into your solar plexus and chest as well.
- Exhale through your nose, and feel a sense of releasing tension down through your buttocks and feet as you feel your energy sink deeply into the earth.
- As you inhale, you may want to think, "I am strong and grounded."

- As you exhale, you may want to think, "I am relaxed."
- If you like, you can visualize red, the color associated with the root chakra, as you breathe.
- After focusing the breath in the belly, allow your breath to start deep in the belly and expand into the diaphragm and chest, as we do in Abdominal Breathing.
- As you close your eyes and continue the Earth Breath, inhaling through your nose and exhaling through your nose, observe your thoughts, emotions, sensations, or any images that come to mind.
- How does it feel to breathe the Earth Breath? What do you notice or observe?

DRAWING IN EARTH QI

Now, let's add some qigong to our earth-based breathing practice.

- If you were sitting, stand up, feet shoulder-width apart and knees slightly bent.
- Tuck your tailbone a bit so it's pointing to the ground, allowing your spine, neck, and head to align with ease.
- Let your arms dangle in front of you, your fingertips pointing down to the earth.
- Gently continue the Earth Breath, inhaling through your nose and exhaling through your nose.
- Bending your elbows and wrists, fingers still pointing downward, slowly raise your hands, imagining each fingertip drawing earth energy up through the fingers into your arms and shoulders, as well as through the soles of your feet and into your legs and belly.
- As your wrists reach chest level, slowly flatten your hands, palm facing the earth, as if they are floating on the qi in front of you. Hands are parallel to the floor and wrists straight.

- As you exhale, lower your hands back down slowly and gently, as if your hands are floating down.
- Near your belly, let your wrists rise and hands drop back into the fingers-pointing-down position, perpendicular to the floor or earth.
- Repeat the drawing up of earth energy as your hands rise and the releasing as your hands drop down. Repeat this three or four times. See if you can tap into the feeling of soaking the qi up through your fingers (and, by extension, your arms and body) as you inhale, fingers dangling down, and raise your hands; then, on the exhale, tap into a floating sensation, as if resting on qi, as you bring your hands down.
- Now place your hands in front of your belly, or lower dantian, with your palms parallel to the earth, continuing to inhale and exhale through your nose.
- On the exhale, imagine roots growing from the soles of your feet deep into the earth.
- On the inhale, imagine that earth energy rising through the soles of your feet.
- Each time you exhale, imagine your roots growing deeper and wider. Let your roots tap into the rich soil, fresh underground springs, mineral deposits, and even to earth's fiery core.
- As you inhale, with fingers pointing towards the earth, imagine your fingers and legs drawing up the earth energy. From these roots you draw whatever you need: minerals, moisture, warmth.
- Draw up the ability to create things in form, to take heavenly inspiration and bring it to life here on earth in the form of a book, a play, a movie, whatever you are writing.
- Let this energy fill your being.

- Notice how, when you fill your body with earth qi, you nourish your physical and energetic body, increasing vitality and well-being, making it easy for creativity to flow.

WRITE.

- **Sounding Stories**: Close your eyes and breathe. Listen to the sounds around you for five or so minutes. When you open your eyes, record the sounds, spelling the sounds out in whatever way captures them for you. Then work on a larger piece in progress. Or start something new.
- **Groundhog Fantasy**: Imagine yourself tunneling with groundhog:
  - Dig into the rich soil before you begin writing.
  - Tunnel through your unconscious. What do you see?
  - Ingest.
  - Digest.
  - Let your writing project become a part of you.
  - Let go of what doesn't fit. What do you let go of?
  - Allow the writing to come from deep within, from your very cells. Know the writing as part of you and draw from those places within you where it resides.
- **Talk to the Animals**: Imagine yourself in a meadow with the intention of meeting a spirit guide and protector that is an animal (often referred to as an "animal totem"), such as the groundhog I envisioned earlier in this chapter. Close your eyes. What animal comes to mind? What message does it have for you? Write a dialogue with it, follow it on a journey, or just write a story about it. See where it takes you.
- **Set It Up**: Consider the settings in a writing project you are working on:

- Scenes in a novel
- Scenes in a memoir
- In a self-help or how-to book, the space where an anecdote takes place
- The landscape of a poem or shorter piece
- The current situation in a business proposal

Ask yourself how you can use the setting to reveal information about characters, theme, your mood, or other aspects of the work. Even if you are writing something short, like a blog post, is there a way to bring a sense of place to the writing? Can you start with a story, a specific place in a moment in time? For example, is the yard coming back to life after winter, reflecting the sense of ease returning to a household after a trauma?

BREATHE.

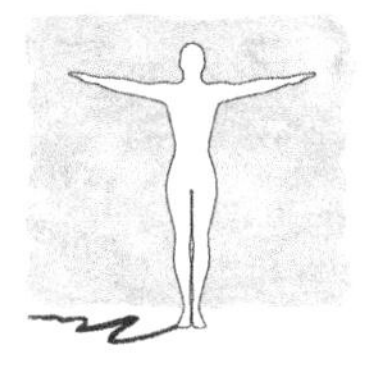

Return to the Earth Breath, inhaling and exhaling through your nose. Smile and feel gratitude for the earth that supports and sustains your life. Bring your hands to your heart. Aloud or silently, offer a one-word prayer of thanks to the earth. Close your eyes and ask for one thing you can do today for the earth. What comes to you? Can you do it immediately or commit to do it at a specific time today?

In the next chapter we will explore the Water Breath, and you can compare the qualities stimulated by Earth Breath and Water Breath, as well as the experiences that unfold with each.

CHAPTER 11

Attuning to Nature with Water Breath

"Nothing is softer or more flexible than water,
yet nothing can resist it."

— Lao Tzu, ancient Taoist philosopher

I sometimes struggle between the pull of life's many responsibilities and my inherent need to feed my heart, soul, and body through time spent outdoors. Nature often provides exactly what my psyche needs to shift gears, inspire new thoughts, delve into writing again. Nature offers physical, mental, emotional, and spiritual energy—all of which feed creative work. I do my best writing when the energies are vitalized and in balance.

BETWEEN THE WORLDS

An hour west of San Juan, Puerto Rico, along the Dorado coast, I lie next to my husband in a king-size bed in a condo by the beach. The sound of peepers and hundreds of birds—cooing, hooting, howling, chirping—fills the night. They chorus loudest in the lush greenery overtaking the former hotel next door and the adjacent hurricane-swept timeshare buildings, the roofless tiki bar, the remnants of a towel shack.

Drifting in a twilight state, I recall images of the day—a saucer-sized orange-red hibiscus, its sticky yellow stamen advertising delectable nectar. The intermittent rain that made murky puddles between the tree roots marking our climb to the second waterfall in El Yunque National Rainforest. Bright mud splattered across my calves, my new pants, my shoes. The chilling rush of waterfall, drilling into my head, face, and chest. Images and sensations come one by one, unbidden.

I fall asleep to the crashing of waves and forest chorus of peepers and birds, breathing in the warm, moist Caribbean air.

When I immerse myself in nature, my monkey mind turns off. Lying in bed, instead of scattered thoughts and anxious projections, my mind returns to the strongest impressions of the day—snippets of memory—visual, auditory, tangible, and kinesthetic. Recalling the mud, I experience the physicality of it, as well as its essence. As if, at night, each element of experience returns to me to reveal a deeper nature, inviting me to know the muddy step, my foot, the hard, protruding root that provides a foothold, my connection to this concentrated moment, and my experience as both observer and observed, as separate, connected, and One—all at the same time.

This transition moment between wake and sleep gives me a second chance to experience my day, ironically in a more awake state than my so-called waking state. This brings to mind the Chinese philosopher who pondered whether he was a man dreaming at night of being a butterfly or a butterfly dreaming of being a man.

As we cultivate an expanded sense of who we truly are—through concentrated time in nature, through the breath, through the practices in *Breathe. Write. Breathe.*, we discover that we are not the busy thinking mind that takes over so much of our attention when we give in to its tyranny. When we make space in our experience for the numinous, we truly start to experience ourselves as both the grain of sand and the light of the stars. Everything in nature invites us to experience its essence, not just its external expression. This rapt knowing is fulfilling and joyous. It heals our habits of experiencing ourselves as separate and disconnected from all of creation. This knowing fills us from a deeper well, an infinite creative source of which we are not only a part, but a whole.

When I skimp on movement, nature, writing, or my qigong practice, I snap at the smallest thing. How about you? What activities are essential to your well-being? Are you making time for them daily? When you feel resistance to writing, movement, being in nature, or a spiritual practice, remember that it often takes one small step to return to these life-giving and fulfilling practices.

BREATHE.

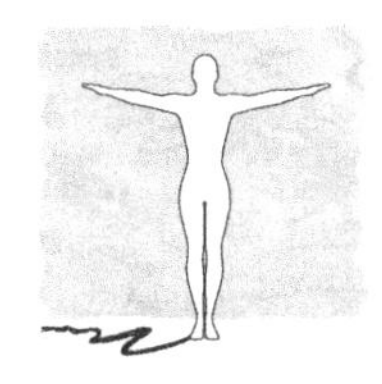

WATER BREATH

Our breathing exercise will focus on the Water Breath.

The Water Breath relates to the second chakra, the sacral chakra, located three fingers below your navel, like the lower dantian. Think of the qualities of water to understand this chakra and breath. Water is the universal solvent. Water cleanses and heals. Water connects to our unconscious, our dreams—both sleeping and waking. Use the Water Breath to stimulate imagination, to connect with the symbolic world, to explore the sensual and sensory world. Second chakra houses your sexual organs—it is home to fertility, creation.

The Water Breath—in through the nose and out through the mouth—can put you in a dreamy state, particularly if you breathe continuously without pause. Use the Water Breath for cleansing your body, mind, emotions, and spirit. Use the Water Breath to release blockages or stale energy, and to heal. Use the Water Breath to activate creativity.

You can read the instructions or let the audio recording guide you.

LISTEN TO THE MEDITATION:

Water Breath

https://lisatener.com/water-breath

WATER BREATH

- Sit in a comfortable position.
- Remember that breathing from deep in your belly, as well as your diaphragm and chest, brings the greatest benefit to your whole body.
- Place both hands on your belly, just below your navel, over your second chakra.
- Inhale through your nose and expand your belly into your hand.
- Exhale through your mouth with a sigh, and imagine releasing all physical discomfort and stress from your body.
- On the next inhale, allow the breath to expand your lower belly, then solar plexus, and chest. Feel the breath expand against your sides and back as well.
- Do 3, 6, or 9 rounds of inhale and exhale, feeling your whole belly expand on the inhale—front, sides, and back of the belly. Feel a deep release as you exhale.
- With each breath, imagine the inside of your body becoming more like water, liquefying, as if you are the water given form by your body.
- You may wish to add the water hand position (mudra), to activate water. Fold in the index, middle and pinky fingers of both hands and bring the tip of your thumb to the tip of your ring finger. (Note: I use the hand gestures taught by Dr. Randolph Stone in

Polarity Therapy. You may find other hand positions called "water mudra" elsewhere, and this position called something else. Both are correct, just different traditions.)

- Rest the back of your hands gently, comfortably on your thighs. Each finger is associated with an energy pathway in the body, the tip of the finger being a receptor for that flow. By joining the thumb (ether) and ring finger (water), you activate the water energy and water pathway in your body.
- As you close your eyes and continue the Water Breath, inhaling through your nose and exhaling through your mouth, observe your thoughts, emotions, sensations, or any images that come to mind.
- How does it feel to breathe the Water Breath? What do you notice or observe? How does it compare to the Earth Breath you practiced in the previous chapter?
- Continue to practice the Water Breath as you imagine clearing and releasing blockages, including any stagnation in your writing or creative life.

WRITE.

MERGE WITH YOUR WRITING:

- If you like, write down a few questions you have about an ongoing writing project or about your writing, in general.
- Imagine yourself floating down a river, letting go of cares and "shoulds." Release the desires of the ego, and let your mind, body, spirit, consciousness just drift, carried by the current. Imagine yourself coming to a spit of land or a dock along the river. You stop there. What do you see, smell, hear, and sense?
- Is there a message here for you today?

- Breathe the Water Breath, inhaling through your nose and exhaling through your mouth. Imagine yourself merging with and becoming the piece of writing you are working on (the poem, story, article, post, or book, for example—or your writing, more generally). With each breath, you merge with the writing itself. Experience your writing project as alive, within you, as a breathing being, radiant with life.
- What is it like to embody your book or writing project? Can you feel a deeper access to the material? Take a few more Water Breaths, and relax into this new perspective.
- If you have questions about the work, feel free to ask them of yourself now and see what comes up as a response. If no questions, you can still see what arises in this space of being the writing.
- When you open your eyes, note your observations and insights. Use this Water Breath as a gateway to a work in progress. Alternatively, see if any of the images or observations inspire you to begin a poem, short story, business proposal, screenplay, or other new piece. Feel free to use any of these prompts for additional inspiration:
    - Write something about water. Anything.
    - Write about your writing project from the perspective of *being it*, using "I" as if your project is talking.
    - Explore an image or metaphor from your watery journey—through poetry, short story, or through the eyes of a character in your writing.

Or try one of these prompts:

- **Writing Snippets**: Go outdoors. Yes, now. If you're in a city, find green space. You can do this practice sitting in one spot or walking mindfully. Notice the natural life wherever you are—vegetation, insects, birds. Allow yourself a moment to take in each life form you see as you inhale through your nose. Exhale through your mouth and relax your gaze while keeping it on the same thing. On the next inhale, imagine taking in the essence of what you are looking at. Exhale and release. Vary your perspective from a wider-lens view to a narrow focus on one thing—a leaf, an ant, a grain of sand. Then bring the lens back out to the bigger picture.

Now find a place to sit and write snippets of what you remember, describing your impressions from the practice. No need to make sentences. Just immerse yourself in the experiences as you write; allow the writing to be a catalog of impressions. When done, read over your impressions, pausing to recall whether you left anything out. If so, dive deeper. What else surfaces? Is there meaning that wants to be made of the experiences? If so, explore.

- **Color Your World**: Go for a walk in nature, or walk throughout your home. Look for a color that catches your attention. Tell the story of that color using all of your senses except sight (or with less emphasis on sight if you need to include it).

BREATHE.

Return to the Water Breath one more time, inhaling through your nose, exhaling through your mouth. Allow your "mind to enter the breath, and the breath to enter the mind," as my qigong teacher Leah Franklin often instructed us to do in class. "Be" the Water Breath. Allow the breath to breathe you, without thinking about what that means and just letting the breath take over. Imagine yourself entering the river of consciousness, much like the Buddha, who sat by the river until his consciousness merged with the river.

CHAPTER 12

Playing with Sound, Space, and Inner Portals

"Music in the soul can be heard by the universe."

— Lao Tzu, ancient Taoist philosopher

IN THE BELLY OF THE WHALE

Two gongs clang and clash, loud vibrations dancing around each other—dissonant, resonant, dissonant. They break up my stagnant energy, which eventually settles down, as if the particles of my being rearrange themselves in a more harmonious order.

I'm lying on my back on a green tatami mat in the barn at Laughing Hummingbird Farm. Michael Robert Pieranunzi, the father of my son's friend Julius, has offered me a "gong bath." In this type of meditation, one bathes in the healing sounds of one or more large gongs, as they vibrate and resound in one's ears and body. It's a penetrating experience. The sounds are loud, not always pretty. Some people say that the gongs break up energy blockages and release tension.

The space itself is otherworldly. They no longer make barns this large without trusses. The openness and height—nineteen-foot ceilings—create the sensation of being in a cathedral. The shape of the ceiling resembles the upside-down hull of a ship. A space that takes you places.

I close my eyes. At first thoughts arise and intrude—lists, worries, goals. As I let each go, another comes to take its place. My thoughts peel off, one by one, until my mind relaxes and I drift, allowing snippets of experiences and impressions. I awaken to a sense of having entered a portal where time, space, and even dimension, fall away, providing access to an expanded sense of who I am in this vast universe we live in.

As I open my eyes, I see the vaulted ceiling through new eyes. The shape of the space brings to mind the belly of a whale, the curved ceiling beams, a whale's ribs. I am Jonah in the belly of the whale, surrendering to my spiritual nature, swallowed by the Divine.

The space feels both real and unreal. I share this with Michael Robert who feels it too, the sense of the vast and formidable inner work within the whale that transforms us.

TWENTY YEARS OF TRUST

On another visit, Michael Robert offers the story of his friend, a devout Buddhist Monk and Aikido teacher (sensei), who told him, "For twenty years I meditated every day and nothing happened."

"Nothing?"

"Nothing. Yet, one day, after twenty years, it clicked."

Most of us receive at least a few glimpses of what's possible as we take up a spiritual practice—enough to encourage us to remain on the path. If your spiritual practice doesn't seem to be working, remember this sensei. If your writing seems weak, falls short of your expectations, remember this sensei. If you feel tempted to skip your writing time because you don't feel inspired today, remember this sensei. Put in the practice—for both your spiritual and writing routines.

I think of this sensei, from time to time, to help me recommit to my writing practice, especially when I need to be more consistent. We may not see the results we want every day that we write.

You may not love what you wrote yesterday or today, but if you practice consistently, you will reach a point where everything clicks, just as it did for the sensei. You may be back again the next day to a feeling of disappointment. Stick with it. Writing isn't always fun. Of course, we love when it is, but the days of slogging are just as important. Let the sensei serve as another portal to your creativity—one that encourages you to trust in the process and stay committed no matter what.

So stick to your practices, but don't become a slave to routine. Sometimes, our resistance is telling us something new. Maybe the practices we use no longer work for us. Maybe we need to mix it up. Maybe we need a smashing gong to wake us up and rearrange the very molecules of our existence!

Sound can reorganize us on a vibrational level. Sound cleans out the cobwebs, reveals possibilities, and creates space for the new. Sound offers a way to shed our rote perspectives and to open ourselves to the numinous, surprising, and spontaneous in our creative projects. Such a portal can bring us into an inner realm where we think and perceive differently.

In addition to sound, interesting spaces (like the barn I described) can also act as portals that transport us into new creative territory. When we combine sound and space, we can alight upon even more transformative experiences. My friend Katja Esser sings in caves. She is one of the most innovative and prolific people I know—a multidisciplinary artist, painter, mask maker, ceremonialist, teacher, performer, and healer. Ever experimenting with sound and sacred space, her work is a prime example of the hyper-creativity one can access through these modes or portals.

Consider how you might incorporate sound and interesting spaces to infuse new life and innovations into your writing. You can experiment with singing, chanting, or prayer to create an inner portal wherever you find yourself. A cozy nook or a vast cathedral-like space can add a magical element that transcends the mundane and infuses your writing with power. You can incorporate other senses into your portal experience by lighting incense or candles.

You can also play with sound in your body. Notice how the vibration of sound within your body serves as a type of portal that carries you beyond the everyday. Today, in our breath work, we will explore sound and space as ways to travel beyond the concrete physical world and visit new landscapes—inner and outer.

BREATHE.

BREATHING MEDITATION WITH SACRED SPACE AND SOUND

For this meditation, I suggest you have something at the ready to write with when you finish—a digital device or notebook and pen. Also, set up the recording of the gong bath so it is ready to play. Read through and follow the instructions, then play the gong bath audio led by master sound healer, Tamara Monosoff, Ed.D.

LISTEN TO THE GONG BATH:

Gong Bath

https://lisatener.com/gong-bath

- Find your portal: Find any space that feels conducive to transporting you to a higher state of being—a spot in nature, a room in your home, or a liminal space between the inner and outer such as a sunroom, porch, or gazebo. You can even sit in a doorway.
- Sit in your portal and breathe the Earth Breath: Sit in a cross-legged position. Inhale through your nose and exhale through your nose, if possible. If your nose is stuffy, see Chapter 7 for a method to clear your sinuses.
- Breathe deeply: Breathe into your lower dantian. You may place a hand on your belly and notice as your breath raises and lowers your hand with each inhale and exhale.

- Feel your earth connection. As you sit and breathe, feel your connection with the earth, the support of the earth.
- Listen to the short gong bath: Relax your body and let the sound wash over you. If you prefer, you can move from a seated position to lying down on a mat with a blanket over you. With each breath, feel your body relax further. Feel the vibration of sound within your body.
- Continue: Let your deep breaths rise and fall. As thoughts arise, acknowledge and release them, returning to the sound and vibration within.
- Sit in silence: After turning off the sound, continue to sit in silence for a minute or longer.
- Variations: You can search YouTube for sacred sounds that appeal to you—Native American or Japanese flute music, bells, crystal bowls, etc. If you have your own bowl or gong, feel free to use that. In fact, if you can do this with a friend, you can each try this exercise by playing for each other—one makes sound while the other meditates, then switch.

WRITE.

Choose one or more of these prompts to play with:

- **Write Sound**: If you feel inspired, write a short poem, essay, or story inspired by your experience of the sound meditation you just did. You may want to start by trying to translate a sound into letters and put that sound at the top of your page.
- **Write Through Your Portal:** Imagine a dark, womb-like space, or a vast and open space like the barn at Laughing Hummingbird, or any sort of portal to other scenes, other lives, other spaces, or other ways of being. Describe the portal. Imagine that you open a door in the portal, and describe what you see beyond it. What unfolds in the new time-space-dimension before you? Write about it.

- **Portal Scene:** Write a portal scene in your work in progress (or start a new piece with a portal scene), perhaps a scene that moves from one space into another, or one state of consciousness into another—or both!
- **A New Path Opens**: Enter your Inner Garden as in Chapter 5. Find a path you have not taken before. Perhaps this path ascends a mountain or goes deep into an underground cave. Explore.

BREATHE.

During my first group gong bath at Laughing Hummingbird Farm, Michael Robert invited guests to start each day by looking into a mirror, directly staring into your own eyes, and saying, "I am beautiful." Create your own writing affirmation, such as "I am a prolific and creative writer" or "I am a writer whose work brings love and beauty to thousands of readers." Do it now. Look in the mirror, into your own eyes, and say these words. How does it feel to affirm this to yourself in the present tense? ("I am…") Can you commit to this practice daily?

You may also want to express your gratitude to your inner muse through sound. Sing a prayer of gratitude or a love song to your muse. Or just close your eyes and make whatever sounds come, offering them to your muse as a loving acknowledgement of your creative source. You can also read aloud the piece you just wrote as if you are sharing it with your muse, with love and gratitude.

CHAPTER 13

Dream Work as Creative Inspiration

"All individuals are profoundly creative because we all dream."

—Kari Hohne, polymath, dream shaman, recording artist, author, and founder of Café au Soul

THE MAN WHO LED ME BACK TO DREAMING

Many years ago, my first substantial conversation with my future husband focused on dreams. When we met, Tom managed the Cowley Fathers' bookstore at the Episcopal Diocese of Massachusetts, and I ran a nonprofit organization, Hospitably Homes, which placed families of patients traveling to Boston for medical treatment into the homes of volunteer hosts. The Episcopal Diocese provided office space for the nonprofit.

Everyone in our building attended an anniversary celebration, where Tom and I got to talking over a glass of champagne. Tom told me about a book he had been reading, *Where People Fly and Water Runs Uphill* by Jeremy Taylor, which teaches readers to tap into the power of dreams for healing individually and in community through starting a "dream group."

As Tom described his intriguing dream of fishing, a common spiritual metaphor, I could picture him on the shore, fishing rod in hand. His dream seemed evocative, alive, filled with promise. All I could remember of my own dreams? Some variation on this theme: I'm back in school, usually college. I'm late for a class I've never attended and can't find the room. It's the end of the semester—the final exam—and I've done none of the homework and attended zero classes. I feel a sense of panic.

The possibility that I might actually dream other dreams than the panicked school nightmares—and that I could learn to remember and record them, mine them for gold—this stirred me.

Once Tom and I began dating, we put together our own dream group, one of the most powerful and intensely creative experiences of my life. Our group shared dreams twice a month. We helped each other understand the many layers of meaning, celebrate aha's and insights, enjoy the humor of dream symbols and subconscious puns.

This dream work fed many activities in my life: healing from a chronic illness, deepening my relationship with Tom, writing and publishing a book with one of my dream-group buddies Peaco Todd, writing poetry, solving problems that had to do with work, understanding myself and my life purpose more clearly, feeding my mind/body/spirit. There was no end to the richness of the dream work.

DREAMING THE ARTIST WITHIN

After going on a women's retreat in Jamaica led by women's studies scholar Marianne Connor and artist Pat O'Brien, I dreamed I was leading a workshop in Jamaica. When I shared the dream with Pat, who had become part of our dream group, she invited me to teach a workshop with her in the very same cove where we'd snorkeled and made pottery months earlier. The result became "Dreaming the Artist Within," where we led a group of women for a week of creating art and writing. We shared our dreams and their possible meanings, incorporating the dream symbols into our writing and artwork. Pat dreamed up the idea of creating dream shields with paint, cardboard, and materials found on the beach, which incorporated the symbolism and meanings we drew from our dreams throughout the week.

This workshop with Pat was my first foray into the kind of creative, experiential teaching I do today. Over a decade before I became a book writing and publishing coach and teacher, my dreams were preparing me for my career and life path with a taste of the work I would later claim as my passion.

Nowadays, recording my dreams serves as a portal into writing. I often wake up, walk through the night's dreams in my mind, then reach for pen and journal and record what I recall in detail. The dreams often inspire several poems, or sometimes an article, blog post, book chapter, or even a possible new book. The images and subjects of my most powerful and evocative poems come directly from my dreams.

REMEMBER YOUR DREAMS AND TAP THEIR POWER

Do you want to tap into the transformative and creative power of your dreams? The exercises in this chapter will be easiest to work through first thing in the morning—just upon waking. Our dreams usually begin to slip through the net of consciousness as soon as we wake up. The sooner we write them down, the more we remember. If you're reading this later in the day, consider reading the dream recollection tips below, then practicing this chapter's breathing and writing exercises first thing tomorrow morning.

Here are some tips to remember your dreams, most of which I learned from Jeremy Taylor, author of *Where People Fly and Water Runs Uphill*, still one of my favorite books on working with your dreams for insight, growth, and healing:

- When you go to bed, tell yourself, "I am going to remember my dreams when I wake up."
- You may also want to have a penlight or headlamp by your bed in case you wake up in the middle of the night and wish to record your dreams.

- Have pen and a journal or notebook by your bed to record your dreams. While you can use a phone or tablet instead, the digital device is much more likely to keep you awake afterwards. I suggest you reserve electronic devices for morning recording only, if at all. I also find that the act of writing by hand is more conducive to remembering dream details and to staying in a creative state of flow.
- When you first wake up, stay in your sleeping position and ask yourself, "What did I dream?" If only a little bit comes, or just a small impression of the feeling, write it down. If, however, you remember large parts of the dream, you may want to mentally revisit the dream in its entirety and then write it. Experiment to see what works best for you.
- When recording my own dreams, I sometimes make one-word notes in the margins to remind me of various details so I don't forget them.
- Jeremy Taylor suggests that if you still have trouble remembering your dreams, try lying in different positions and ask, "What might I have dreamt in this position? How about this position?" I have used this advice to remember dreams when I thought I'd lost them.
- I recently learned a wonderful technique of making a rough sketch of the dream from the book *Drawn into the Dream* by Walter Berry. Just reading a chapter from Walter's book often leads to particularly poignant or powerful dreams. A few months after finishing the book, I reread it just to stimulate my dreams and creativity further.

BREATHE.

ABSORB YOUR DREAM WISDOM

You can do this exercise just after recording a dream or any time at all, with or without a specific dream in mind. However, I encourage you to try it first thing in the morning if you are able. Listen to the audio meditation Absorb Your Dream Wisdom.

LISTEN TO THE AUDIO:

Absorb Your Dream Wisdom

https://lisatener.com/absorb-your-dream-wisdom

- With your hand on your lower belly, take a few deep breaths. You may wish to use the Water Breath, inhaling through your nose and exhaling through your mouth.
- Imagine the wisdom of your dreams sinking into your very being.
- As you inhale through your nose, feel gratitude for your dreams—the wisdom, healing, creativity, direction, inspiration, spiritual connection, and personal growth they offer you.
- As you exhale through your mouth, feel a sense of peace.
- Breathing in, connect with your dreaming self.
- Breathing out, allow that connection to deepen.
- Feel gratitude for your dreaming self, for the symbols of your dreams, and for the energy you connect with as you dream.
- Take several breaths here as you continue to imagine your dream's wisdom filling your consciousness, in whatever way feels authentic to you. For example, you can imagine white or golden light filling every part of your body.
- If it feels right, make a commitment to remember your dreams. Place a reminder on the wall of your bedroom to cue this when you first wake up.

WRITE.

DREAMING THE WRITER WITHIN

PART I: AWAKENING

- Do you have a yearning to pull your covers up over your head and snuggle back down for more sleep?

- Do you ever wake up shivering and find your top blanket on the floor?
- Do you wake up alert and ready to leap out of bed?
- Write about your feelings and observations. Write about your experience waking up in this room, this body, on this day, after these dreams, whether you remember your dreams or not.
- If you feel resistant to writing down and exploring your dreams, explore that.

PART II: TIPS FOR RECORDING YOUR DREAMS

- Use present tense as if your dream is happening in this moment.
- Write on every other line so that if more details arise later, you can fill the blank lines. Or leave a big margin on the left side of the paper.
- You may remember your dreams in a different order from how you dreamt them. I often make notes afterwards to show myself the order in which I dreamed. If I originally recalled them and therefore wrote them down in a different order, I may put brackets around the scene I dreamt first and label it "A," the second one "B," etc. Often, the first part I remember is the one closest to waking. If I transcribe the dreams from paper to computer, I will use the notations to put the dreams in the order I dreamt them, to help with interpretation and the movement, growth, or shift that the dream progression might suggest. You may find that you can't remember the order or that scenes seem to have happened simultaneously. Dream coach Kari Hohne once told me this is a sign you're especially in touch with the illusory nature of time—well done!
- As you write, you may often remember additional scenes or dreams. If they flow too fast to capture everything, make notes in the margins to capture some of the symbols.

PART III: INTERPRETING YOUR DREAMS

Once you record a dream (now or first thing tomorrow morning), see if you can discern any messages.

- Does the dream offer insights about your writing, your creativity, or your life?
- Does it seem to offer you a choice or guidance?
- Does it provide insight into a book you are writing? A character's back story? A new scene? A new chapter?
- Are there puns or layers of meaning that add depth to the message?
- Feel free to dialogue with a dream character or symbol. You can ask the character/symbol questions about meaning and purpose, such as "Who or what do you represent?" or "What do you want me to know?"

If you don't remember a dream now, when you prepare to write first thing in the morning, as you breathe deeply, see if you can remember a dream from the previous night. Use the tips on the previous page for remembering dreams. It's okay if you don't remember any details. Even connecting with the shadow of a dream can connect you to your dreaming self and its fluid access to rich imagery.

After writing observations, dreams, or dream dialogues, open up to wherever the writing takes you. Free associate, write a poem, write about a problem you are trying to solve, make notes for a character you'd like to know more about, or develop an exercise for your creativity book, as I do here.

WRITE MORE.

If you're working on an ongoing writing project, first thing in the morning (after recording your dreams) is a particularly fertile time to immerse yourself in that project. If not, see if the dream provides a jumping off point for a poem, essay, or story. More ideas:

- **Explore** your dream scenes and symbols. Do they offer metaphors, structure, or insights into any writing project you're working on?
- **Dialogue** with a character in your dream. Or dialogue between a character in your dream and a character in the work you are immersed in, which can prove especially fruitful in uncovering the fictional character's motivations, secrets, and history.
- **Try a rough sketch** of one of your dreams, drawing one or more scenes. Explore any insights from the illustration.
- **Note any symbols or dream characters** that particularly captivate you from a recent dream. Explore associations you have with the symbol or character. Then look up the symbols in Kari Hohne's online dream dictionary at cafeausoul.com.

BREATHE.

Take a few deep belly breaths before you move on to the next thing—appreciate a moment of stillness in your day. Inhale through your nose and exhale through your mouth, using the element of water (Water Breath) to acknowledge the watery qualities of the dream state, the unconscious mind, and the creative aspects of our being.

Feel the luxury of not rushing into another activity and, rather, enjoying a pause to feel grateful for your writing practice and for your dreams. End your practice with a breath of gratitude. Breathe in a sense of abundance and gratitude. Breathe out and acknowledge the many gifts of your breathing-writing practice. Cultivate gratitude for your deepening relationship with your dreams, which can feed your writing and other aspects of your waking life.

Before you go to bed tonight, you may want to invite your dreams to answer questions about your work or to help you explore themes and symbols in your work. You can even put a note under your pillow stating your intention or asking a question of your dream self.

CHAPTER 14

Freeing Up Stuck Emotions for Deep Writing

"If you don't live it, it won't come out your horn."

—Charlie Parker, American jazz musician and composer

When aspiring authors tell me they're blocked, I often find they need support to express themselves. As we explore what's holding them back from full self-expression, common themes emerge: parents who told them to shut up, a teacher or other adult who said they were a poor writer, or experiences in which speaking up caused punishment, embarrassment, or harm.

Upon closing their eyes and scanning their body, many writers who feel stuck notice tension or discomfort in the area of the throat. Some folks even find their body communicating to them in the form of illness. Artist Yvonne Parker offers a remarkable story of healing a blockage to self-expression and a related physical illness.

HOW YVONNE FOUND HER VOICE

Yvonne is a bold multimedia artist, interior designer, and art seller with clients all over the world. Over lunch with my family, she told us that six years earlier she had developed a goiter. The non-cancerous growth on her thyroid grew so big that it pressed against her vocal cords. Her doctor suggested draining it to see if it disappeared, which she tried. Within a month, though, the goiter grew back and her doctor suggested surgery.

Looking for a nonsurgical solution, Yvonne asked the goiter, "What do you want to show me?" When she turned her attention inward, she heard, "Express yourself through your voice; speak up for yourself."

Yvonne often hesitated to express what she sensed and felt. Public speaking especially intimidated her, as English is her third language. However, the goiter motivated Yvonne. She joined the organization Toastmasters, prepared speeches, and shared them in this supportive environment. "I learned to speak up and be loud; that was my breakthrough. I spoke my truth and expressed who I am."

Yvonne's Toastmasters presentations landed her a thrilling new job teaching about modern art on a cruise ship. Yvonne and her husband circumnavigated the globe three times, selling art in East and Southeast Asia, Alaska, South America, the Caribbean, and the Pacific. The goiter has never returned, but her adventures continue.

EXPLORING THE ROLE OF THE FIFTH CHAKRA—THROAT CHAKRA—IN WRITING

In the energy system of yoga, both public speaking and writing involve the fifth chakra, the energy center in the throat, where blockages can interfere with self-expression. Deep breathing naturally opens the throat chakra and frees your voice, especially if you work with sound to support that opening.

Just as Yvonne used her goiter's wisdom to free her voice, you can use pain or challenges—physical, emotional, or even spiritual—to access your voice as a writer. If you're feeling blocked, exploring any discomfort—particularly pain associated with the throat, where voice originates—can help you unblock and free up your creativity. Breathe consciously, sing, hum, or make a spontaneous sound to clear this chakra, and you will be amazed by how your voice can shift and creativity flow.

FOLLOWING THE PAIN TO FIND YOUR VOICE

You can also experiment with pain as a way to give your writing voice more depth: In fiction, you can create a character with a distressing problem similar to yours. In a memoir, your pain provides powerful entryways for healing and catharsis for you and your readers. Even in a self-help or how-to book, exploring pain points in your anecdotes can provide a transformative, immersive experience for readers. As bestselling author Brené Brown has taught us, stories that reveal our vulnerabilities draw readers into our work and make them feel as if they know us. Revealing pain and other vulnerabilities creates a relationship with your audience that can make them lifelong readers—and sharers—of your work.

A note about exploring pain in writing: Just focusing on pain will not create a fulfilling experience for your readers. Your writing needs to include moments of transcendence throughout—whether through transformation, humor, or the beauty of the writing itself. If you struggle to gain a perspective bigger than the pain, inner work can help. Some approaches that help me shift are writing poetry, writing in nature, laughter, reading something humorous the night before I write, or exploring my dreams and their meanings, including asking for a clarifying or healing dream.

BREATHE.

I adore the song of spring peepers. When I hear peepers while driving, I roll down my windows and pull to the side of the road to soak in their music, eyes closed. The sound transports me. To me, the peepers' chorus is the voice of the Divine, the voice of God. Peepers—and frogs, in general—are often associated with the throat chakra, the energy center governing self-expression and breath. What a perfect guide for our breathing and writing practice.

RESTORATIVE HALF FROG POSE

Have you ever tried "frog pose" in yoga? This modified version, half frog, is restorative and easy for beginners. It helps counter the effects of too much sitting by opening the hips and gently stretching your chest and shoulders. As such, it's a wonderful antidote for the side effects of writing or typing at a computer for extended periods. You can practice half frog before sitting at your desk to write, during a break from sitting, and at the end of your writing/typing session. Watch the video to guide you in practicing restorative Half Frog.

WATCH THE VIDEO:

Half Frog

https://lisatener.com/half-frog

HALF FROG

- Lie face down on a rug or yoga mat.
- Slide your right leg up so that your thigh forms a 90-degree angle with your torso and another 90-degree angle with your calf.
- Relax your feet.
- Create a similar position with your right arm, so that your forearm forms a 90-degree angle with your torso and another 90-degree angle at your elbow, palm facing down.

- If you need support under your legs or arm, use a folded towel to make yourself more comfortable.
- Turn your head toward your right arm (use a folded towel under your head if needed).
- Imagine breathing into your back body—lower back, middle back, and upper back. Feel your back and sides expand on the inhale, releasing on the exhale. When we breathe deeply, we often focus on the front of the body. Yet the back takes so much abuse—sitting in a chair much of the day, poor posture, etc. By breathing into your back, you can counter the effects of these bad habits.
- Relax in this position for two minutes or more. Notice how you can use your exhale to release and relax more deeply.
- Slide your right leg back to meet the left, release your arms to your sides, and turn your head to the left.
- Repeat the exercise on the opposite side of your body, sliding your left leg up at a 90-degree angle and left arm up.
- After two or more minutes of half frog pose on your left side, release the pose. Slide your left leg back down and place your hands under your forehead, one over the other, cradling your forehead.
- When you're ready, lift the feet toward the ceiling, knees bent, thighs on the floor, and gently windshield wiper your legs by moving your feet from one side to the other. This relaxes your back and releases any tension. You can do this windshield wiper motion for three minutes or more. When done, bring your legs down and keep your hands at your forehead. Just rest, breathe, and notice how your body feels.

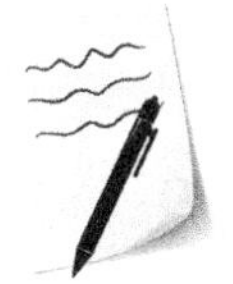

To write truth, we need to tap into the emotions and experiences at our core.

WRITE.

Choose one or more of the following exercises, which connect to the throat chakra, voice, and self-expression.

- **Dialogue with Frog or Throat Chakra**: For example, ask Frog (or your throat chakra) any of the following questions. Then breathe and write the answer, possibly with your non-dominant hand or in a different color ink (blue for throat chakra or green for frog!):
    - How can I explore or play with voice in my manuscript (or a new work or exercise)?
    - What emotions may be stuck in my throat chakra and how can I access them?
    - What should I know about a particular character and their voice; are certain emotions conveyed by their voice?
    - What body messages are here for me today? What do you want me to know?

Use the above questions as a starting point and continue to ask questions based on the answers you receive.

- **Echo Nature**: Getting out of your linear mind and doing something a little wacky with your voice can free up your creativity and open you to novel discoveries, adding new timbre to your voice in the world and on the page. Try this. Go outside and listen to the sounds you hear in nature or in your environment. Imitate the sounds with your voice—a bird song or rustling leaves—then write down an approximation of that sound. City noises work too—construction sounds, a siren, car motors. Have fun opening up to everything your ears can pick up, with no goal other than immersing yourself in listening, voicing, and writing. Then use one or two of the sounds as the start to a poem or story. Write these at the top of the page and go from there. Even if you remove the sound later, starting with it may open up something new in you and your writing.

- **Body Messages**: Breathe in and out, noticing what area of your body calls for attention through sensation. What does it feel like? Is there a shape, color, or sound that comes to mind? If there's a sound, make that sound. Continue, as if you are inhaling directly into and exhaling from that place in your body. Then ask what message it has for you. Continue to breathe into the area. What happens? Is there a shift? You can also ask that part of your body what it needs from you.
- **Finish This Sentence**: Write at the top of your page: "If I could write anything I want..." Write about what you'd write. Then write it!
- **Read Aloud:** Read your work aloud to someone you trust. Notice what comes up as you read. Pause to take notes as insights and ideas arise during the reading process.
- **Listen:** Or have someone else read a piece you've written aloud to you. Note where they may hesitate or misunderstand the syntax. Take notes as their reading reveals ideas for change.

BREATHE.

Taking deep breaths and, originating sound from deep in your belly, sing all or part of what you have written. Have fun with it.

How do your breathing and singing infuse the writing? Do they give you an expanded sense of your creativity, expression, or personal power?

If the exercise inspires any further steps, carry on, but you don't need to do anything except enjoy the playfulness of this exercise and the sense of your creativity being more expansive than you may have realized.

CHAPTER 15

Writing Incognito and Other Tricks to Beat Resistance

"Creativity is inventing, experimenting, growing, taking risks, breaking rules, making mistakes, and having fun."

—Mary Lou Cook, author

RESISTANCE AND PERSISTENCE

I don't want to write today. I missed two days last week and am quite familiar with the ease with which a precious habit can slip away. Yesterday, I ate a large peanut butter cookie and a banana nut muffin. Neither tasted that special—the cookie, greasy and overly sweet; the muffin, not banana-y enough. That didn't stop me. Nor did my frequent sneezing as I brought dairy and sugar back in my diet for the fifth day in a row. Now, sweets have become the new habit.

The groove of not exercising has crept up on me as well. Days passed without a walk or qigong, so my writing routine is the only good habit I'm clinging to right now. Precariously.

Maybe my problem is thinking I may be close to the end of my current writing project, yet feeling unsure of what's missing. I believe I should type up my handwritten chapters before I can know what I need.

On the other hand, some mornings I feel certain I've gotten it all down, nothing left to write, then a new insight comes to me when I make the time for writing.

Now, I realize I forgot my breathing practice today, so I take a few breaths from deep in my lower dantian. Earth Breaths—in through the nose and out through the nose. I lie in bed and practice a Sinking Breath, another practice I learned from Leah. I imagine inhaling through the pores on my skin, exhaling as I let my consciousness sink deeper and deeper into the earth. Join me if you want. I feel more grounded already. How about you?

Yesterday I planted herbs and flowers. I sank my bare hands into the rich, organic potting soil from Earth Care Farm in Charlestown, RI. Now, as I practice the Sinking Breath, I re-experience that rich earth, alive with minerals and qi. My being easily slips through the recently tilled soil, down into the sulfur-rich hot springs and crystal-studded caves of my imagination.

CHOICE POINTS AS TRIBUTARIES: WHERE'S THE FLOW?

Unexpectedly, my husband enters our bedroom and plops on the bed, where I am writing in my journal. Tom sighs, then pats the bed loudly for Sophie, our Labradoodle, to join us. Instead, she wags her tail loudly against the radiator, the clanging joining the bed patting and Tom's entreaties to "Hop up, baby."

I had hoped to embark on a deep inner journey with my writing and here we are on a noisy bed. There was a decision point where I knew I could probably get back to that inner cave, where man and dog would take my cue and settle down, but I chose to go with my surroundings.

Now I ask myself, "Where's the juice, the aliveness? In the clanging, wagging, patting, entreating mayhem? Or deep in the earth?" Finding aliveness guides me in my writing choices.

We may come to our writing with some idea of where we want to go. Sometimes it flows like a river in early spring. Sometimes the river forks. There are choices to make. Follow the main river or check out this little tributary?

We may have an unwritten rule in our heads saying, "This doesn't belong," but what if it does and we just haven't made the connection yet? You won't know unless you explore the tributary.

The good news is, you can backtrack. Maybe this curious character is a distraction. Perhaps that scene didn't belong. Maybe I'll cut the chapter I'm writing this morning and no one will ever read it.

Writing is not just about the destination. We need to be willing to explore, to kick around, to see what lies on the surface and what hides in the dirt, too—even if you dig it up and then refill the hole with nothing to show for it. Somewhere, someone has buried the gold coins. Once in a while, you find them. I'll see what happens with the chapter I'm working on; does it stay or go? Either way I kept my habit. I stayed open. I'll call it a win. Happily.

Maybe I'll even jump on the rebounder. First, I'll bask in the glory of being a writer who writes and breathes deeply.

MIMI AND THE WIG: BE AN ADVENTURER

Jumping on the rebounder, I think about rules and breaking them. This reminds me of a story—another tributary, I suppose—and I'm not sure it bridges so well, but since it's about breaking all the rules, here goes…

My golden-haired mother-in-law Mimi has put on a wig of long, curly, black hair. She looks like someone who might start howling at the moon, perhaps because of the bizarre disconnect between her pale skin, blonde eyebrows, and the ebony hairdo. My husband, who shares her coloring, tries on the wig next. Somehow, it works on Tom. As he eats his bowl of ice cream, he looks like a 1970s rock star, a cross between Slash and Howard Stern, back in Stern's long-hair days.

Mimi tells us the story of her wig. She arrives at a yoga center during the birthday bash of its founding guru. She had called ahead and heard they were full. Always up for adventure, she chances it, the excitement of being up close to the guru during the festivities proving irresistible.

The person at the front desk confirms they have no space for her, but somehow Mimi feels sure she'll find an extra bunk bed in one of the shared dorm rooms. She leaves, concerned that if she tries to sneak back in, the desk people will recognize her. Not to be deterred, she drives into town, procures a long-haired black wig, and dons a pair of dark sunglasses. Not a snazzy wig, something you might pick up in a Halloween store if you wanted to look like a mean old witch—itchy, scraggly polyester. In the parking lot, a guy twenty years younger tries to pick her up. This part of the story has us in hysterics because, despite being a beautiful woman, she truly looks insane in this get-up. That's this guy's type, huh?

Mimi describes sneaking into the yoga center, merging with a group that had just finished a meditative hike. She's in! She snoops around the dorms, making a mental note of a bunk bed with no personal belongings on it. After dinner, with everyone settling down to sleep, she sneaks in and climbs to the second bunk.

As she's drifting off—black wig still on her head—her lower bunk mate pokes her from beneath, "Hey, you weren't here yesterday. My friend was supposed to be in that bed but got sick and bailed." Mimi mumbles back a response, feigning sleep.

The next morning, used to the wig by now, she skips off to early morning yoga. All's fine until downward dog when her wig slips; she holds onto it for dear life during sun salutations and manages to keep the wig in place for the rest of the weekend. This story entertains our entire family for years to come.

Mimi was a rebel, if someone said, "You can't," she heard, "You need to find another way." To Mimi rules were made to be broken. Her orientation led to zany adventures, some of which would give me an ulcer. To her they provided adrenaline, a thrill, new experiences, and a spontaneity to life. Her rebellious nature contributed to her impressive success and fulfillment as a painter and sculptor.

When I get too staid in my patterns, Mimi offers the contrast of stepping out of my comfort zone, my perspective, or my habitual ways of seeing and being in the world. She offers a way to get beyond limitations and discover something new.

INVITE THE TROJAN HORSE

And this brings us to the Trojan Horse. The Greeks needed to get into the city of Troy to win the ten-year war. How do you get into a place you're barred from? Be tricky, like Mimi, right?

Let's say some part of you—maybe your inner critic or the self-doubter—is the Trojan, barring the writer from some area you want to explore. That self-doubt shows up as resistance. And you can't just push your way in. Maybe, though, you can get in there disguised as a giant wooden horse! If the critic bars your way, disguise your writing as seemingly harmless. Write about a man and dog on a bed. Just start describing what's around you, which can lead you inside where the curious thoughts lie, where the past can be explored. You just have to sneak in there with something seemingly benign.

In other words, go in now, in the present, describing something around you, and you'll find your doorway into the sometimes elusive secrets of the past, or the caves of your psyche where you've yet to explore. Who knows what you'll discover—a humorous streak you didn't know you had? An inner character ready to be given voice?

Today's breathing practice may be a Trojan Horse. It's certainly a deviation from our habitual ways of breathing. And so there's the promise of discovery. Something new. Are you up for it?

BREATHE.

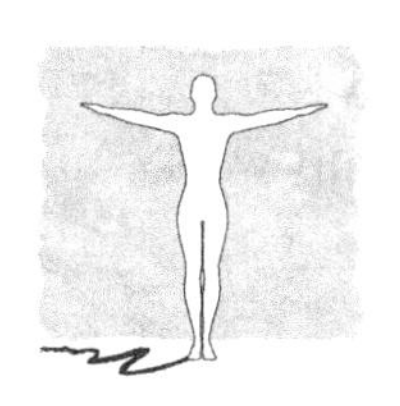

Listen to the audio to Breathe Like a Star.

LISTEN TO THE AUDIO

Breathe Like a Star

https://lisatener.com/breathe-like-a-star

Today we begin with a simple practice I made up. And I confess, I found it a lot of fun! I hope you do, too.

- Stand with your feet shoulder-width apart, your knees unlocked, your tailbone gently tucked. Tense your shoulders up to your ears and then relax them with an "ah" sound. This shoulder relaxation is something that my qigong master teacher Robert Peng includes whenever we begin our practice. Robert also teaches us to gently tuck the chin and raise the back of the head as if someone is pulling you up by the hairs on the crown of your head. Smile and relax your jaw. Robert says the smile is the most important part! That and "Have fun!"
- Now that you're in a ready position, close your eyes and imagine that you are a star in the sky. Imagine the brilliant light at the center of your being as you breathe in. Imagine radiating your light as far as the inner eye can see as you exhale.
- Take 9 breaths like this, breathing in from your center and exhaling as you shine. Become the light of the star.

"Creativity involves breaking out of expected patterns in order to look at things in a different way."

—Edward de Bono, physician and author

WRITE.

Choose one of these exercises or come up with your own:

- **Cleansing**: Write about a cleansing experience

you've had, such as cleaning a closet or house, or feeling cleansed after time in nature, for example.

- **Letting Go**: Write about letting go of a relationship, person, or object. This can be fictional or non-fiction.
- **Be a Star**: Imagine you are a star in the sky. Write from the voice of the star. What arises?
- **Light Headed**: Write a poem or short prose about a head that fills with light. Imagine the process and see where it takes you.
- **Thwarted Character**: Close your eyes and breathe deeply. If you're working on a fiction piece, think of a character and imagine them being thwarted in their desire, being told, "No." Imagine your character putting on a disguise to skirt the rules. How do they do it? What rule are they breaking? How do they act differently when dressed this way? Write the scene.
- **Disguise Yourself as Your Character (Fiction or Nonfiction)**: Put on your own disguise: get a wig and pick out some clothes from the Salvation Army, something you'd normally never wear. Go somewhere incognito—a restaurant, a mall, or a park. Get into character and experience life through the character's eyes. What would they do? How do they interact—or not—with the strangers around them? Write a scene, using your real-life scene or making up a new one. How does it feel to play an alter ego? Can you incorporate this new perspective in your writing, either in a particular piece or in general? (If you can't get out, just imagine the scene and write about it.)
- **Break the Rules of Your Usual Form:** If you tend to write free verse poems, choose a structure. If you write fiction, try an essay or a cookbook recipe.
- **Take a Step**: Start like I did early in this chapter. Just describe what's going on around you. See where it leads you.

- **Trojan Horse**: Imagine hiding inside a Trojan horse. What are you trying to sneak into? What's your Troy? What do you discover inside?
- **Decision Points**: Write about some decision or choice you need to make at work, in your writing, or in relationship. Use the breathing exercise from this chapter (or another favorite) to relax and open to new ways of seeing your choices/decision. List possible options or perspectives you haven't thought of before. Explore.

BREATHE.

Return to any calming type of breath such as Earth or Water, as you cultivate a sense of gratitude for your experience. Explore any insights you discovered during this chapter's activities. Have you explored new inner territory? Tried something experimental? How can you continue to push the usual boundaries? Is there an exercise you can include before or during your writing practice? If so, commit to using it next time you write. Make a note about it in your writing notebook or calendar.

CHAPTER 16

Breathe Like a Toad

> "I believed then—in a deep, easy way that is impossible for me as an adult—that there was more to this world than meets the eye. Trees had spirits; the wind spoke. If you followed a toad or a raven deep into the heart of the forest, they were sure to lead you to something magical."
>
> —Jennifer McMahon, author

This spring has been particularly overcast and cold. My antidote? I fill every flower pot and hanging basket I can find in our cellar and place them on the porch. I plant pink and purple hyacinths; lemon yellow, rosy pink, and psychedelic purple tulips.

I come to the large pot with the fairy house last, a birthday gift from my children. The shoebox-sized house sits on stilts atop the oversized bowl-shaped flowerpot in which my boys originally planted yellow and purple Johnny Jump Ups, baby clover, and a purplish green miniature leaf. Last year, I planted magical looking Lemon Drops. Today, I pull a few weeds and wonder if the tiny seedlings with the bumpy leaves are Lemon Drops or Creeping Charlie. Keep or pull? I decide to wait a week and see if I can better discern.

I turn my attention to the fairy-sized landscaping. A stone path from the edge of the pot to the fairy house has scattered, and I reassemble it. I dig out the tiny bench and place it upright. I peer through the fairy house door to see what's inside—a miniature porcelain dog and an even smaller bottle of blue glitter. I lift the house out of the flowerpot and shake it to free the items from their hiding place.

As I lower the house back into the flowerpot and place the dog by the bench, a flicker of movement catches my eye. Inside the fairy house, a small lumpy thing—visible through the window, now completely still—blends in with the grayish material of the inside walls.

A closer look reveals a toad, facing away from me, easy to miss. I marvel at his ability to turn a color I've never before seen on a toad—the gray-white of concrete.

His magical appearance delights me. My more linear mind, though, wants to figure out where he came from. Close inspection of the house reveals a small space between the floor and wall of the house on the right side. I find it hard to imagine him fitting through so tiny a space.

In seated position he looks twice as fat as the fairy house door.

I return my attention to the seedlings and Creeping Charlie, then a few minutes later, look back into the house for my toad. He is gone. No way could he have hopped out of the little house without my seeing him. I try peering into the crack between wall and floor, but make out nothing.

The toad stays with me in spirit through the day, his appearance and vaporization leaving a residual sense of the magical. His invisible presence becomes a surprise gift I carry with me day after day. This toad reminds me that, when we pay close attention, we uncover wondrous secrets beneath the surface of things. This is especially true in our quirky interactions in liminal spaces that bridge the man-made and natural worlds, such as where a fairy house in a pot meets the great outdoors.

I smile from time to time as I think of Toad over the next few days. I attempt to peer into the space between floor and wall again, but can't discern anything. I believe he's still there, making his hidden home in our shared fairy house.

TOAD MEDICINE

When I do some research, I learn that toads have nearly 360-degree vision. Toad can teach us about looking at the bigger picture, seeing beyond our everyday perceptions. They help us expand our viewing capacities.

Similar to Frog, the connection between Toad and voice, or self-expression, comes to mind. Toads make a variety of loud sounds, from musical trills to harsh buzzing and guttural creaking. I am struck by both their range of view and range of expression.

As amphibians, toads also teach us about living in different environments and distinct phases—watery and earthy. As writers, we also travel among different planes—the symbolic, watery dream world; the earthbound world of the senses—and states of consciousness. Toads, too, symbolize fertility and creativity. Toad seems a fitting animal totem, or guide, with many lessons to teach a writer.

THE TOAD IN THE DRAIN PIPE

My connection with magical toads goes way back to childhood. When I was eight and my siblings four and six, we stayed in a motel in Miami with my parents and grandmother. A large drain pipe by the pool curved about nine inches above the ground. Over several days, we kids observed both a family of toads and several large pink palmetto bugs popping out of the pipe and exploring nearby. Most of the time, however, one palmetto bug and the largest toad kept watch, perched together inside the opening for hours. They guarded the entrance like sentinels, within a couple inches of each other. I imagined them as the daddies, protecting their families in the pipe. Toad and Bug seemed to enjoy a congenial relationship, and I wondered how they communicated across species.

Children often move through life with less of a controlling, I-have-to-get-things-done attitude than adults, and more of a natural openness to the world around them. Perhaps that is how I came upon Toad and Palmetto Bug in the first place—my child self's open eyes. Would I have missed this as an adult?

As writers, we would do well to return to childlike observation and sense of wonder, paying attention to the fantastical world around us. What goes on in the drain pipe and fairy house can be so much more interesting than the superficial world we see when we rush about getting things done.

BREATHE.

TOAD BREATH

As amphibians, toads breathe through their lungs and their skin. The idea of breathing through your skin may seem foreign, but many qigong practices employ it. Shall we give it a try?

LISTEN TO THE AUDIO

Toad Breath

https://lisatener.com/toad-breath

- Lie down comfortably in a space that has nurturing energy, perhaps your bedroom, a sunroom, the living room.
- As you inhale, imagine breathing through the pores of your skin along the entire surface of your body. Fill your chest cavity and lower dantian as you breathe in the nourishing qi around you, envisioning that it enters the surface of your skin and moves throughout your body.
- Imagine exhaling through your skin as stale qi leaves your belly, diaphragm, and lungs.

- Now focus on a particular part of your body. It could be a part you rarely think of or an area experiencing discomfort. It could be something you see, like a finger, or something you can't see, like an organ or cell.
- Breathe into that particular part of your body. Imagine that you breathe in through the skin of, or around, that body part, and you exhale through the skin as well.
- Notice any observations in a gentle way.
- Continue this practice of inhaling and exhaling through the skin and into your body.
- After several breaths, you can move your focus to another area of your body, "Skin Breathing" once again.
- When you feel ready to end the practice, return your focus to your whole body and skin breathe through the surface of your entire body. Do this for several breaths or as long as you like.

What is your experience?

"A good writer possesses not only his own spirit but also the spirit of his friends, *including animals, plants, rocks, and any of the loving, living beings around us.*"

—Friedrich Nietzsche, words in italics Lisa Tener

WRITE.

- **Seek the Quirky in Nature**: Go outside and look at things with an openness to small details. Peer into places you don't normally look—under a rock or leaf, in a water drain, at the back of a tree, under the porch, in the bushes, in a spot of grass the size of your hand. What can you discover? Now bring that level of detail to your writing. Describe a scene or person, looking for curious details. If you are writing fiction, allow for something magical to appear. If you are writing nonfiction, be open to a mystical dimension, as well. Let your expanded senses be a gateway for discovery as you write.

- **Skin Breathing**: An Inquiry
  - Follow the instructions for Skin Breathing again, focusing first on your whole body and then on one body part.
  - Now ask that body part one or more questions—straightforward ("Tell me about yourself.") or off-the-wall ("Neck, what's it like to hold up my head?").
  - Write the answers that come.
  - Feel free to stick with the exploration or move on to an ongoing project.

- **Be Reptilian**: Practice Skin Breathing. Lie on the grass or the beach. A rug works as well. Alternatively, you can stand in a relaxed position, feet shoulder-width apart, knees slightly bent. As you breathe, imagine inhaling through your skin and exhaling through your skin. Imagine your breath evenly distributed throughout the skin of your whole body. Experience expansion and contraction as you breathe in and out. Imagine your skin becoming scaly, reptilian. Become a reptile. Write about your engagement with the world from your new perspective.

- **Breathing into Character:** Inhale and exhale through your skin, as in the previous exercises, imagining that you're becoming a character in your novel, short story, or memoir. Which character? What do you learn about the character? Now write a scene from that character's point of view.

- **Magical Creature:** Imagine a magical creature that hides in your yard or home. Describe it. Go on a journey with it, and see where it takes you and your writing.

BREATHE.

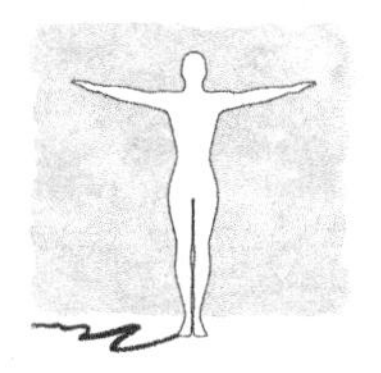

When you complete your practice, sit somewhere outdoors or in a room with many windows, where you can take in the outdoors. Perhaps you even want to crouch or squat like a toad, knees splayed and hands flat on the floor in front of you. Feel gratitude for Toad magic, for the nature that surrounds you, and for your writing practice.

As you continue to breathe naturally, experience yourself as part of nature. Imagine yourself like the magical toad whose skin tones change with its surroundings. Allow your breath to connect you with everything you see, as if with each exhale you release your hold on who you believe yourself to be and you merge with the air, the soil or grass or sand, the life around you. With each inhale, take a bit more of your surroundings into your body.

Close your eyes and continue to merge with nature. Open your eyes when you feel ready. If you like, and if you're squatting like a toad, take a few toad-like hops forward. How does it feel to leap into the next part of your day or evening?

CHAPTER 17

Surrender, Trust, and Creative Flow

> "True freedom is when all the stories, all the insights, all the realizations, concepts, beliefs and positions dissolve. What remains is what you are: a vast, conscious, luminous space simply resting in itself, not knowing a thing, at the point where all things are possible."
>
> —Enza Vita, spiritual teacher and author

FROM SICK AND ANGRY TO HEALTHY AND CREATIVE

One night many years ago, I lay in bed feeling like I needed to shed my skin or run away. An intense anger and frustration seemed lodged in my body, along with a sense of powerless. I didn't know what to do with it, how to get rid of this distressing sensation. I certainly couldn't fall asleep.

At the time, I was studying Polarity Therapy. In our training, we viewed emotions as energy. Anger, in particular, was considered "fire energy" in this system.

What if I imagined this anger I felt as powerful fiery energy coursing through my body? I enhanced the exercise with the practice of "Fire Breath," inhaling through my mouth and exhaling through my nose, the way I imagined a fire breathing dragon might! The powerless feelings melted away as I got in touch with this potency within me. Wonderful, except that now I couldn't sleep with all the fiery energy coursing through my veins.

Feeling these waves of energy, I got out of bed and an idea formed: a book to help people experience their anger as a teacher and tool. Anger as messenger. Readers just needed the right tools to shift their experience. The tools? Their creativity, sense of humor, inner wisdom, and the exercises to help them tap into those tools for transformation.

Back in my bedroom, I grabbed my journal and pen, and began writing that book. It took seven years and two amazing co-authors for *Good and Mad: Transform Anger Using Mind, Body, Soul, and Humor* to be published by Health Communications, and one more year for the book's final incarnation as *The Ultimate Guide to Transforming Anger.* I had no idea that this fateful night of imagining my anger and frustration as fiery energy, would plant the seed for a new career as a book coach, which emerged—or sprouted—more than seven years later.

Polarity Therapy helped me inhabit my body, not just my mind. It opened the window to a spiritual life. It gave me back my health and helped me realize my childhood dream of becoming an author. Then it went beyond that to help me create a career I did not know existed. I re-invented myself as a Creativity Coach, which evolved over time to Writing Coach, then Book Coach.

I wonder what these Polarity exercises will do for you.

As we've explored, much of Polarity work begins with breath. To try Fire Breath, breathe in through the mouth and out through the nose a few times. Interesting, right?

BREATHING LIFE INTO YOUR CREATIVE ENDEAVORS

Why does the breath work so powerfully for creative pursuits?

We know that deep breathing calms the mind and relaxes the body. And there is more. In this relaxed state, we can be open to not knowing. When we feel tense, we want to control things. When we relax, we can trust. Trust leads to creative breakthroughs and compelling writing.

When we relax and trust, magic can happen:

- We write a poem, or two, or three, or more.
- We fall in love with someone so different from what we imagined as a fit (me with a religious person? Really?)
- We find our own personal cure for an illness—and realize the illness delivers a message about what we were missing, and offers the gift of a more expansive, happier world view and spiritual life.
- We find new ways to be in our bodies.
- We realize our dreams.
- We discover a new character for a short story or novel.
- We hit upon our next book idea.
- We create; we write; we publish.
- We find purpose.

Really? All that from our breath?

Yes.

Breathe deeply, stop defending, relax, let go of what you know. Open your heart to what the work—your essay, your poem, your book—yearns to become, wants to teach you, and you have more to offer your readers as well.

It's a so-so book at best when it's all about what you, the author, already know. Your book can live up to its full potential when you open to the unknown. When you relax:

- What metaphors arise?
- What stories?
- What qualities come forth?
- What new connections do you make in the work? What insights emerge?
- In what creative ways do you fully engage your readers?

2D BECOMES 3D AND "LIVING COLOR" GOES PHOSPHORESCENT

We all have a Control Freak in us. As writers, our job is to decide how much that freak gets to control. Give the Control Freak a job—to choose the form, to make an outline, perhaps. Then breathe. When the Control Freak finishes its job, thank the Control Freak. Let it know it did a good job with the outline. Now it can enjoy a little vacation while you surrender to the creative process. You'll need its help again when you're ready to edit, not now.

Orient yourself away from the Control Freak and toward the Creative Muse by taking a deep breath. Breathe to give your work:

- Spontaneity
- Authenticity
- True authority
- Power

This open attitude can be especially helpful if you feel at all stuck or frustrated. By being curious, you create space for something fresh to happen in your writing life. Ask "What if…?" often.

Creating from this place, you, as a writer and a human being, transform. When you transform, your readers ride that wave with you, whether it's explicit or not. Your openness is a gift to your readers. Your transformation is their transformation.

BREATHE.

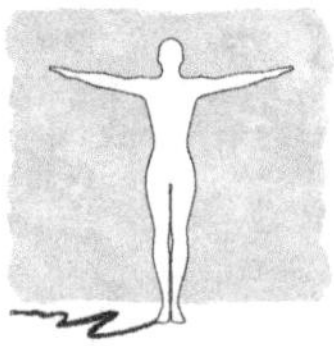

KNOCKING ON THE DOOR OF LIFE

This next qigong practice is a staple warm-up. It gets your energy moving and stimulates the "ming men" or "the door of life" energy point on your spine, directly behind the navel. The practice also energizes the central nervous system and stimulates the kidneys, an important storage and management center for vital life force energy. Kidney energy is associated with water and creativity—an extra bonus for those of us using this practice to prepare for writing.

WATCH THE VIDEO

Knocking on the Door of Life

https://lisatener.com/knocking-on-the-door-of-life

KNOCKING ON THE DOOR OF LIFE

- Stand with your feet hip-width apart.
- Turn to the right and swing your arms gently as they follow along with your torso, letting your left hand wrap around to tap the right thigh, as your right arm swings behind you, your right hand tapping near the left buttock. Some qigong teachers describe the arms in this practice as akin to ropes that swing out when you twist. My friend Jane suggests "empty coat sleeves" swinging.
- Turn left and swing your arms to the left, letting the right arm tap the left thigh while the left arm taps the right buttock from behind.
- Continue to swing back and forth, 6 times on each side.
- Now bring your hands up a little higher and let them wrap around the waist, the back hand tapping the point near the spine which corresponds with your navel or kidney area, repeating 6 times each side.
- Lastly, turn right and tap your right shoulder with your left hand, while the back of your right hand taps your left kidney.
- Turn left and tap your left shoulder with your right hand, while the back of your left hand taps your right kidney. Repeat 6 times on each side.
- Slow down and allow your arms to swing more gently with each turn, until you come to rest.
- Close your eyes, breathe deeply, and observe how you feel.

"If you trust yourself, you can step into the world of unpredictability without a clear picture of the outcome. In fact, you learn that you can be more creative when you discover it as you go. Take an interest in living your life as an art form. This kind of creativity is needed in today's world more than ever before."

—Dr. Patricia Hoy, conductor, musician, and author

WRITE.

"What if…?": Write a few notes about where you think a piece you've been working on is going next. Or if you're not working on a piece, just jump in. Either way, write "What if…?" and list ten or more ideas—as out of the box, unrelated, or fanciful as possible. Feel free to include a few less fanciful ideas as well.

Underline the ideas that show promise and pick one to try out. Expand upon the "what if" in relation to a project you've been working on, or on its own as a standalone piece. See where it takes you.

Here are a few examples to get you started, in case you need them:

- What if this took place ____________ (in a cupboard, on another planet, in Switzerland) instead?
- What if this character (isn't really human? secretly hates/loves ______? holds a secret?)
- What if I'm looking at this all wrong?
- What if I invited my readers to ____________?
- What if I tied this story to ____________?

- **Magic Carpet Ride**: Close your eyes and breathe deeply or try one of the many breathing practices you've learned in *Breathe. Write. Breathe.* Imagine traveling on your breath, like a magic carpet ride. Where does it take you? Describe the journey and any resting places on the way. Write the question "What's my destination?" Answer the question. Or feel free to have a specific destination in mind; ask to go there; and allow your breath to take you. What do you see, hear, smell, sense, and discover?

- **Fire Passion Poem:** Imagine your creative energy as a fiery passion. Describe it in a poem. Let its voice emerge. What does it want you to know?
- **Find a Story**: Go for a walk in nature. See what grabs your attention, preferably something you can pick up. Look at it and breathe deeply. Place it in your other hand and do the same. Place it back where you found it. Now tell its story. When you feel done with your writing, ask yourself whether you've incorporated all your senses. If not, explore the senses you missed and see if you can add them to the story. Remember that we are not always going for a piece to polish. Writing can also be about developing your craft, exercising new muscles, exploring various tools for the process. If that is the case, let that be enough.
- **What If? at Work**: Are you a bit of a Control Freak at work? Write about ways this may be true. Then imagine someone in your workplace who seems more relaxed, easy to work with, or flexible. Write about how you imagine they might deal with the things you are trying to control. What might be the new outcomes?

BREATHE.

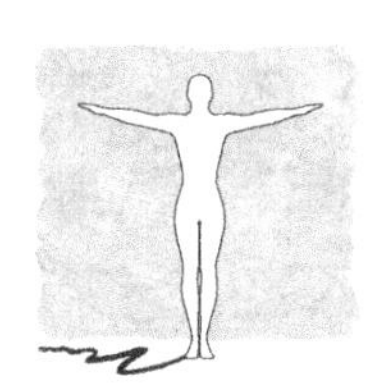

Repeat the Knocking on the Door of Life a few times. Notice how it feels after writing. Do you detect any changes in ease, tempo, or other aspects of your experience?

Now take a few deep, slow abdominal breaths to transition, perhaps the Earth Breath (in through the nose and out through the nose) or Water Breath (in through the nose and out through the mouth).

CHAPTER 18

Owl Wisdom

"Return to the mind that is restful and curious, perched just beyond the outskirts of the universe."

—Kari Hohne, polymath, dream shaman, recording artist, author, and founder of Café au Soul

When my husband Tom and I began dating, he took me to his mom's house one weekend and invited a couple he knew. As the four of us walked down the road, I spied an owl, high up on a branch in a distant tree. "Look, an owl!"

"Where?" Carol asked. No one else saw it until we walked much closer.

"That's not an owl," Steve said. It clearly looked like an owl to me.

"It's too exposed to be real. It must be a plastic owl to scare away the birds," Tom offered.

I decided he must be right, but Steve tested the theory and threw a rock at the leaves near the owl, causing it to stir. Owl, indeed. And alive. (But, come on, Steve. Who throws a rock at an owl? Just no. Don't do that.)

I have an uncanny sense for seeing animals in nature, animals that normally hide from humans or disappear in the light of day. I believe we all have this ability when we open our awareness to the previously hidden world around us, the world that our harried, productive, modern selves insist we don't have time to explore. It takes quieting our mind chatter and slowing down to natural rhythms for us to see this world.

On one level, the owl incident immediately showed me that not only did I discount my knowing, but I stifled my voice and didn't speak up when Steve threw the rock, despite how wrong his actions felt to me.

My interaction with the owl continued to reveal a new understanding about my life. As I recalled the owl while lying in bed that night, I had a kinesthetic experience. I felt myself on one side of the owl, representing divine feminine energy, and Tom on the other, representing divine masculine energy. The owl perched above us in the center, as we wound around each other like ribbons on a maypole. I felt the power of this interweaving of masculine and feminine. It conveyed to me that every romantic relationship has a dimension greater than the experience between two people. In our off-kilter world, each relationship holds a healing power to balance and harmonize feminine and masculine.

This understanding was not so much a linear thought; it came as more of a felt sense, full mind-body-spirit kind of knowing.

Although we'd only been dating for a couple of weeks, through this experience with Owl I knew Tom as my soul mate, our relationship as part of our personal healing and a planetary healing. This may sound grandiose, yet many cultures view the everyday world as full of symbols and guidance.

Life speaks to us through symbols that help us learn, grow, heal, and create, if we slow down and listen. Jesus spoke in the symbolic language of parables as did many prophets of the Hebrew Scriptures. The Hindu stories in the Bhagavad Gita and other spiritual texts are meta-metaphors, full of symbolism.

When I walk a client through my Meet Your Muse exercise, the muse often speaks through symbols, both by how the muse shows up (and in what guise) and by providing symbolic images in answer to our questions.

PAYING ATTENTION TO SYMBOLS IN YOUR LIFE

Pay attention to what you see and hear today:

- Animals that cross your path
- A word you hear several times from different sources
- Song lyrics that pop out
- Sensations or pain in your body
- Objects or people that spark something within you
- Numbers that show up repeatedly

If each experience appeared in a dream, how might you interpret the symbols? First tap into your intuition for answers. After that, you can look up symbols on the internet. Kari Hohne's dream dictionary at cafeausoul.com is my favorite resource.

What does the symbol or symbolic event have to teach you about your writing or other areas of your life?

You can also seek a symbol. You can close your eyes, ask a question, and see if a symbol comes up. Or you can find an inspiring animal totem card deck, like Jamie Sams' *Medicine Cards* or the beautiful *Spirit of the Animals* by Jody Bergsma. Think of what you plan to write about today and ask for an animal spirit guide to support you. Or pick a card without any specific plan, and write about what the card means to you or seems to communicate.

USING SYMBOLS TO INSPIRE AND ENRICH YOUR WRITING

While writing is an inner journey, you can add elements of the outer world to make it more concrete. Bring some fresh cut lilacs to your writing space, light a candle, or breathe in the scent of your favorite essential oil. If you have a deck of animal spirit cards or any other divination deck, choose an image that speaks to you and place it in your writing space. These outer prompts serve you in several ways:

- Symbols in your writing space underscore the message that this is your special writing time, connecting you to your creative source.
- These brief rituals connect you with your senses—smell, touch, sight, sound, and taste—the magic talismans for your authentic voice.
- Such brief rituals become part of your writing habit, making it easier and easier to groove right into writing from a place of wonder.
- Simple rituals provide an easy way to bypass the inner saboteur.
- Rituals can add an element of fun and play. And the muse loves to play!
- Writing rituals have a way of making our writing time feel more magical. Bringing in symbols can open you more fully to the creative magic within you.

BREATHE.

AIR BREATH

The opposite of the grounded Earth Breath, Air Breath untethers us, lightens us, gives rise to many thoughts. Air evokes qualities of movement, speed. In Polarity Therapy work, air is associated with the fourth chakra, the heart chakra, and the color green.

How will Air Breathing will work for you? Will it give rise to too many thoughts? Or will it open your heart? Take you flying above the canopy? Let's find out.

LISTEN TO THE AUDIO

Air Breath

https://lisatener.com/air-breath

AIR BREATH

- Sit in a comfortable position.
- Remember that breathing from deep in your belly, as well as your diaphragm and chest, brings the greatest benefit to your whole body.
- Place hands on your heart, your fourth chakra.
- Inhale through your mouth as you allow your heart space to expand, throughout your chest cavity and in all directions—frontwards, to the sides, and back to your spine.
- Exhale through your mouth.
- Do 3, 6, or 9 rounds of inhale and exhale, feeling your heart space expand on the inhale—front, sides, and back.
- Feel a loving calm as you exhale.
- You may wish to place your hands in a special position to enhance the quality of air. In Polarity Therapy, we call this "air mudra." Bring together your thumb (symbolizing ether) and index finger (air). Fold the remaining three fingers of both hands into a gentle fist. The ether thumb helps activate the energy represented by the finger it touches.
- Rest the backs of your hands comfortably on your thighs.
- As you close your eyes and continue the Air Breath, inhaling through your mouth and exhaling through your mouth, observe your thoughts, emotions, sensations, or any images that come to mind.
- How does the Air Breath feel to you? What do you notice or observe?

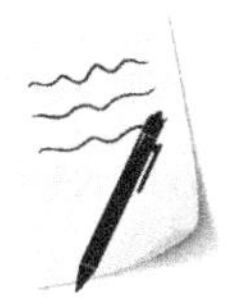

"The act of writing is really the act of coming to know oneself."

—Dani Shapiro (at a Kripalu writing workshop)

WRITE.

Breathe the Air Breath. Breathe nine or more air breaths, in through the mouth and out through the mouth. Then choose one or more of the prompts below. You may want to listen to the following audio meditation/visualization before doing the first or second prompt.

- **Air and Me:** Write about—and explore—your relationship to air.
- **Flight:** Breathe the Air Breath again, this time imagining yourself as an owl or other flying creature.
    - Imagine growing wings.
    - With eyes closed, take a journey in your mind as that creature, flying.
    - When done, write about the experience.
- **Night Vision:** Imagine yourself as a night creature, like owl, or a bat or firefly. Write about what you see with your night vision as you fly through the darkness.
- **Writing Ritual:** Create a writing ritual incorporating the steps below:
    - Choose a symbolic object and hold it in your hands. Feel its weight, shape, and texture.
    - Close your eyes and imagine carrying your sacred object with you as you open a gate to your creative Inner Garden and walk through as in Chapter 5
    - Imagine your object soaking up the good qi of the garden, and being able to bring that good qi back with you in the object, to inspire and support your writing.
    - Imagine bringing back your sacred object as you return through the gate to present time.

- Open your eyes and imagine placing the object near you to nourish your creativity.
- Write about the experience and what the sacred object means to you, and use the writing to segue into an ongoing project or new piece of work, such as a short poem, blog post, or story. How does the ritual affect your writing?
- End the ritual with a feeling or prayer of gratitude.
- If you want a simpler ritual, you can light a candle or smell a special essential oil or flower and imagine it giving off creative energy to support your writing session.

- **Symbols at Work**: Is there a character trait that's holding you back at work or a skill or trait that might help you succeed on a work project (or in your career, in general)? Close your eyes and look for an animal or other symbol that might embody the skills or traits that would help you in this endeavor. Write a dialogue with the animal/symbol. Ask it questions and answer as if you were the animal/symbol. What might you do differently?
- **Changing Perspective:** Take an aspect of what you're writing and imagine moving from one perspective to another. For example, take a bird's eye view of a scene or chapter in your novel and write from that all-seeing perspective, rather than that of the current narrator. Or have two characters trade perspective and play with what they learn. Give a character psychic powers; how does that change things? Experiment here.
- **Writing on Air:** Can you bring the qualities of air (spaciousness, movement, expansion, lightness of being, self-expression) into your writing and pen a short poem or story, or return to a work in progress?

BREATHE.

Return to Air Breath, inhaling through your mouth and exhaling through your mouth. With your hands on your heart, breathe at least nine cycles. Close your eyes and, as you cultivate a sense of gratitude, see if a symbol comes to you as an expression of that gratitude.

Consider walking outdoors as a way to get grounded and transition. Of course, if your walk inspires creative ideas, when you return, feel free to sit down and do some more writing!

If you feel too spacey at the end, add a grounding breath such as Earth (inhale through your nose, exhale through your nose) or Water (inhale through your nose and exhale through your mouth).

AFTERWORD

Your Breath-Powered Writing Plan

> "You don't have to lay out a yellow brick road or a path of breadcrumbs for the qi. It's smarter than you think. It knows where to go."
>
> —Leah Franklin, qigong master instructor

We've breathed and breathed and breathed together, and you've written, written, written. What have these practices brought to your craft? What new awareness do you have about yourself?

At times, it's tempting to grab a pen and just write. You can do that. Yet also remember the power of your breath to relax you, to open your mind and heart to a wider range of possibilities, to expand your experiences as you incorporate all your senses into your work.

As you come to the end of *Breathe. Write. Breathe.*, think about what you want to take away from this book. Is it to have a breathing or movement practice to center and relax you, to open easily to inspiration and creative flow? Is it to support a daily writing habit or ritual that gets you writing in the zone?

Was there one practice, or perhaps several, that you found particularly powerful or easy? Perhaps you want to pick one or more of these and use them regularly. You can schedule them as a prelude to your writing sessions. Another possibility I mentioned at the beginning of *Breathe. Write. Breathe.* is that you may want to work through the whole book again, this time with a friend or writing group.

You're also invited to join me and experience some of my favorite movement and breath practices in our group writing sessions (in my Get Your Writing Done or Bring Your Book to Life® Programs).

Look at which page corners you folded down to remind you of your favorite practices, or any notes you wrote in the back of the book about favorites. Recall a practice that brought out your voice and note it here.

____

- Another that helped you discover more deeply what you wanted to say and how. ______________________________

  ____

- Which practice made it easy to just drop in? ____________

  ____

- Which practices got you unstuck? ____________________

  ____

- Which practices supercharged your creativity? __________

  ____

You may choose one particular practice to employ every time you write, or you may decide to mix it up and choose a breathing practice based on your mood. Perhaps choose a deep belly breath when you feel tense or anxious, a twisting breath when you're tired and need a pick me up. If you feel like giving up on your writing project altogether, become a whirling dervish and spin.

As you look back over the practices, choose a few you would like to incorporate into your regular writing practice. Then fill in your super-powered writing plan.

Some practices I'd like to incorporate regularly:

- ______________________________ Page # _____
- ______________________________ Page # _____
- ______________________________ Page # _____
- ______________________________ Page # _____

NOW BEGIN TO FILL OUT YOUR SUPER POWERED WRITING PLAN

- I will play with the following practice as a regular opening to my writing practice this week: ______________________________

  ____
- When I feel ______________________________, I will try ____.
- When I think ______________________________, I will try ____.

Not sure what to write for the second or third intention? What is your most common emotional state that keeps you from writing or makes your writing low energy? What thoughts do you think when you resist writing?

If you are a writer who starts projects without finishing, if you neglect your writing for weeks or months or even years, I encourage you to become the other kind of writer. A writer who writes. You'll likely need to manage your anxiety about writing and not writing. Guess what? Breathing is perhaps the most potent tool for managing anxiety and relaxing. Start there. Conveniently, all of the practices in *Breathe. Write. Breathe.* lend themselves to calming you.

Choose a practice that keeps it simple, and practice it daily for a week or more. See how it serves you. If you're not sure where to start, try the Healthy Dance, reworded for writing prowess: "I have chosen. Now I write." Or "I am writing. I feel great." Find your own affirmation to chant as you reach those hands skyward and grab your piece of heaven. Remember the four claps at the end of your affirmations.

When you feel ready for change, move to another practice you feel drawn to. As you embrace, adapt, and further experiment with your favorite movement and breathing practices, remember the most important thing—enjoy!

Now that you have some ideas about how you'll get into an inspired state of flow and take some of the *Breathe. Write. Breathe.* practices, with you, it's time to choose when you'll do the breathing/spiritual practices and the writing.

- When I will write (specific time window, such as 2-3 pm):

	MON.	TUES.	WED.	THURS.	FRI.	SAT.	SUN.
TIME SLOT							

Be mindful about when you choose to write. I write first thing in the morning and highly recommend it. Your mind remains in a dreamy state, providing easy access to metaphor, experimentation, expanded possibility, and inspiration. You'll likely feel more relaxed, too. It's often an especially productive and juicy time to write.

- What I'll practice before writing (choose one practice or several to draw from):

- ○ ____________________
- ○ ____________________
- ○ ____________________

- I will work on:
  - ○ ____________________
  - ○ ____________________
  - ○ ____________________
  - ○ ____________________

POTENTIAL OBSTACLES

- What might get in the way of implementing my plan? (Check all that apply.)

  ☐ Self-doubt

  ☐ Fear of ____________________

  ☐ Going to bed too late to get up early

  ☐ Lack of healthy boundaries around other people's needs or demands

  ☐ Losing momentum

  ☐ Other ____________________

  ☐ Other ____________________

  ☐ Other ____________________

- What I can do to prevent these experiences or to nip them in the bud if they do come up (check all that apply):

  ☐ Realize the unhelpful belief or thought and embrace a belief or mantra that better serves me. For example, "I trust my process and write." Write your mantra here:

  ____

  ☐ Set an alarm for going to bed.

  ☐ Set an alarm for getting up to write.

  ☐ Keep electronics and/or novels out of my bedroom.

  ☐ Set healthy boundaries with ______________________,

  ______________________, and ______________________.

  (People who need or want my time/attention.) I will set these boundaries by (sign on door when writing, turning off

  phone, ________________, ________________, and

  ________________.)

  ☐ Other ______________________________________

  ☐ Other ______________________________________

  ☐ Other ______________________________________

Practicing with a person or group holds you accountable. Think of potential people you could contact to see if they want to write together or work through the exercises of *Breathe. Write. Breathe.* together. By working through *Breathe. Write. Breathe.* a second time, with a partner or in a group setting, you'll begin to make these practices your own, continue to derive fulfillment and inspiration from them, and deepen your experience. You'll also find new subtleties about the practices, enjoying new insights and sparking your creativity in fresh ways. If you're not sure whom to connect with, post a flier at your local library or join an online course. Feel free to reach out to me to find out about my online group writing sessions and courses.

- What is my support and accountability plan?

  ☐ Reach out to ________________________________ (names) to see about being accountability partners or forming a group.

  ☐ Post flier at my local library.

  ☐ Ask the librarian about groups.

  ☐ Join or create a meetup group (meetup.com)

  ☐ Ask ____ for ideas.

  ☐ Join Lisa's Get Your Writing Done or Bring Your Book to Life® Program.

- If you are looking to embrace a morning practice, check the boxes below. I will:

  ☐ Go to bed at _______________.

  ☐ Wake up at _______________.

  ☐ Start my day with the following breathing practice:

  ____.

  ☐ Have ____________________ by my bed or go immediately

  to my ____________________ to write.

  ☐ Check in with _________________________ after writing to remain accountable.

- ☐ Write again at ________________.
- ☐ Work through *Breathe. Write. Breathe.* again, this time with a friend such as ______________ or ________________.
- ☐ Other ______________________________________
- ☐ Other ______________________________________

BREATHE.

Find a spot in your home that feels sacred to the muse—a window, a cozy nook, a warm rug by the fireplace. Go there now. Inhale to the count of six and exhale to the count of six. Call to your muse as you inhale. Feel gratitude to your muse as you exhale.

Acknowledge the time you have spent with the breathing and movement practices, and the writing exercises in *Breathe. Write. Breathe.* Note all the gifts your practices have bestowed upon you—your creativity, the writing you enjoyed and produced, the experience of flow, any feelings that arose in your practice. Celebrate your creative journey! Take a few simple, deep breaths. Inhale. Exhale.

As you enter that place of gratitude, acknowledgement, and celebration, see if a word or image pops into your consciousness. You may want to write it down or draw it to remind you of the power of your practices, including that of gratitude.

Now inhale and throw your muse a loud, smoochy kiss! MMMMWWWAAAAHHHH!

A FEW FINAL WORDS

Every day we are responsible for what we bring into the world. How do we treat ourselves? What do we tell ourselves about life? What do we tell others?

Do we bring more love into the world? Or do we cultivate fear, anxiety, anger, confusion, and worry?

There is great power in writing. A wise comic strip character—and many others—have said, "With great power comes great responsibility."

Muckrake all you want, but remember to elevate, too. We need activist writers who provide hope and solutions. You have a choice: you can leave your readers traumatized, feeling powerless and stuck, or you can leave them empowered, engaged, and uplifted. The practices in *Breathe. Write. Breathe* can help you nourish yourself and your readers throughout the creation process.

If you have a question about the practices in *Breathe. Write. Breathe.* or you want to share your experience, go to LisaTener.com/ Breathe, you can also join/visit the Facebook group Write and Create with Lisa Tener or just share your questions or comments on any blog post of mine. As I said at the beginning of our journey together, I will respond.

Most importantly? Breathe. Write. Breathe.

WATCH THE VIDEO

Your Next Steps

https://www.lisatener.com/your-next-steps

LIST OF PRACTICES

MY NOTES

FAVORITE PRACTICES

My favorite practices:

- ______________________________
- ______________________________
- ______________________________
- ______________________________
- ______________________________

If you work with a practice and you decide you want something new, turn to the list on the previous page to easily find another practice.

Feel free to add notes on what you experienced, what you liked, and any challenges that came up.

WRITING PROMPTS FOR ADVENTURERS

I love a book that keeps on giving and remains a lifelong resource. In the spirit of leaving you with opportunities to keep engaging, here are several pages of prompts for your pleasure, play, and pursuits:

- Start by writing nonsense words. See where it takes you.
- Listen to the birds. Imagine what they're singing about and write a response.
- What writer would you love to get to know in person? Write them a letter (that you don't have to send).
- Think of someone you're jealous of or resent. Write an imagined dialogue between you. Allow it to surprise you.
- Smell something—a flower, a fruit, a soap, essential oils. Then write!
- Close your eyes and imagine love pouring down onto you. Open your eyes and pour the love onto the page as you write.
- Why am I here? Explore.
- List five ways you can contribute to others today (or this week). Pick one and explore in writing.
- List your creative goals for this month (or year). Pick one and explore what it will feel like to reach it!
- List five people you haven't thought of in a long time. Write a letter to one (even if they are no longer alive).
- List five wild animals. Pick one and write about their habitat from their point of view.
- Eat something slowly with your eyes closed. Write about it.
- Journal or write from the point of view of LOVE itself.
- Write about water—your relationship to it, a memory, its qualities, a body of water you feel connected to. Explore.

- Journal/write about peace, reconciliation, or forgiveness.
- Remember flying like an airplane as a kid, arms out, head forward? Try it and then write. What happens?
- Close your eyes and imagine meeting your inner muse. What does your muse want you to know right now?
- Start your writing session with gratitude. What happens?
- Approach your writing in the spirit of play! Write about play or just write playfully.
- Start writing by imagining what you want your readers to experience.
- What inspired you this week? Write about what you will do with that inspiration.
- What's a favorite line or quote you've read or heard this week? Write it down and then explore or use it in a poem.
- Picture your reader in your mind as if writing a letter to them. What happens?
- What are you reading lately? Is there anything new you're inspired to try after reading it—a particular tone, an experiment? Try it!
- What's one wonderful thing someone did for you this week? Or something you hope someone will help you with? Or something generous you did for someone else (and how did that feel)? Explore.
- Write about your morning routine. Or the morning routine you think you should have or wish you had. What do you imagine?
- Write about a guilty pleasure.
- If you gave yourself a permission slip to dream big, what comes to mind? Describe the big dream.
- Explore what fuels your creativity.
- Write a poem or essay or story that draws upon the sense of smell or taste.

- What's one thing that your writing, once published, will do for your readers? Is this something you need as well? Or something you needed in the past and found? Explore.
- Imagine one pleasurable activity that comes out of writing and publishing your work. Imagine it in detail with all your senses. Write about what you hear, see, smell, feel, taste, sense in detail.
- Name two or three things getting in the way of writing. Pick one and imagine a wise guide providing insight about, or a solution for, that problem. Write their advice.
- Imagine you write and publish. A reader comes up to you to tell you what your book has done for them. Write the scene and dialogue.
- Think of a place you loved to go as a kid and describe it.
- Do you ever wonder if your writing is making a difference? Explore.
- What will you do today to court your muse? Describe it, do it, come back to the page and explore what happened.
- Write a poem or essay or story about a household object. Be playful.
- Close your eyes and imagine a scene in specific weather and a specific time of day—snowfall at night, mist in the morning, rainfall midday. Then start writing and see where it takes you.
- Write a poem, essay, or story that draws upon an experience of something extreme—extreme emotions, extreme weather, extreme polarity.
- Write a poem or a thank-you letter for your life.
- Send someone a text, email, beautiful card, or letter sharing how they contributed to your happiness or growth. Of course, one can get carried away by this one. Once those endorphins kick in, you may find yourself writing many!

ACKNOWLEDGEMENTS

Thank you to everyone who introduced my previous book, *The Joy of Writing Journal,* to other readers—through your gracious reviews, gifting the book, and sharing it with your writing communities, social media networks, colleagues, teams, friends, relatives, and more. This is how books make it into readers' hands and hearts. A special shout out goes to Robin Kall and Deborah Alfarone. All that support has positioned me to give *Breathe. Write. Breathe.* an even bigger sendoff.

A breath of gratitude goes to Eric Maisel, who handed me the keys to unblock my writing. Big love to my writing coach and developmental editor: Tama Kieves, you helped me stay connected to—and listen to—my muse; your belief in my writing carried me through years of self-doubt and your early feedback kept me on track.

Melissa Sones, *Breathe. Write. Breathe.* needed to shed some serious pounds; you gave me the courage and insight to let go of almost half of what I'd written, infinitely improving this book; your detailed reworking of the first two chapters was miraculous.

Jane Bernstein, your astute line-by-line edits were essential; many times you came to my rescue with more precise and beautiful replacements for repeated words or expressions that fell short, leaving me in awe of your prowess. It is a dream to work with you.

Anne Patterson, your recollections of Mimi's wig adventure added spark to the telling. A thousand thank you's go to Paula Schonewald, who typed parts of this manuscript from my handwritten scribbles, let me know when something didn't sit right, and often offered "le bon mot." Thanks to other occasional typists, my son Will Patterson and neighbor Alice Dunning.

When I found myself past deadline and still struggling with the Introduction and first two chapters, my son Luke Patterson came to the rescue. Luke, you took me to the mountain top for a fresh view!

That same night, my husband Tom Patterson gave me the advice that brought it all together—"Print the beginning, read it, sleep on it, and you'll know what to do in the morning." He was right.

To my publisher, Tamara Monosoff, I am thrilled to publish another book with you. Collaborating with you is a delight. I can count on you when inevitably some technical challenge threatens to derail the process. And my gorgeous cover! I swooned at the sight.

To Dan Thibeault and Portland Helmich, what a pleasure to work with you both again on the videos and audios for this book. Pieranunzi Family, thank you for the gong baths and feedback! Patricia Muehsam, MD, thank you for helping me make the scientific research accessible. Deborah Louth for identifying an auspicious launch date and sharing important insights on Chapter 2.

Thank you to qigong master Robert Peng, who taught me *The Master Key* and the secret to life: "Easy. Relax. Smile." I am grateful to be able to share what you've taught me—it's changed my life; at our teacher training I was struck by the power of this work to change the world.

To all the teachers who came before—the lineage of monks who brought these teachings to us—as well as Leah Franklin, who taught me how to breathe. And to Linda Broadhead and Dr. Vincent Brunelle who continue to teach me nuances of breathing well. To Daisy Lee and The Shift Network, Lee Holden, and other inspiring online teachers. To Doug Jansen who taught me about energy through his Polarity Therapy training program. To Seraina McCarty, who shared angel messages. And to the many other teachers and mentors in my life, including Julia Griffin, Tiffany Masters, Erina Cowan, Linda Schiller, Margo Dussault, Diane Gannon, Rong Zhang, Nancy Graham, Patricia Gilmartin, Ken Robertson, Pam Oatis, Gayle Meyers, MD, Dan Cohen, Pat O'Brien, and my dear friend and prayer partner, Johanna Cremin, Julie Ryan, John McGonigle, MD, Yvonne Parker, and Auntie Tang. Emily Blefeld, the constellation for this book is a thing of beauty!

Thank you to the team that is helping this book reach readers: VA Extraordinaire, Geri Lafferty who has been my right hand for most of my career, marketing guru Carol Lin Vieira, Laurence O'Bryan, and Books Go Social; Howard Van Es (I know I'll be calling on you for something!), and Seth Jacobson for my gorgeous photos.

Thank you to my co-facilitators in Get Your Writing Done—Sharon Burton and Laurie Hunt—and to each member of the program (as of this writing, Michael, Louisa, Gail, Pam, Kiki, Steffi, Elizabeth, Renee, Helen, Amy and all who've come through the doors, written, and published). You all bring wisdom, insights, and inspiration and have sharpened my skills as a teacher of book writing and creativity. I can't wait to read your published books and see them doing their work in the world! Thank you to everyone in our Facebook Community, Write and Create with Lisa Tener and to those who've stepped in to moderate when I could not (Dana McNeely!).

To my writing teachers, the late Frank Conroy, for teaching me to revise and edit; Professor Gjertrud Schnackenberg; my sixth-grade teacher Ms. Schmiemann; Professor Irene Taylor, who introduced me to the poetry and art of William Blake; my parents for their love of books and encouragement.

To beta readers—Joshua Home Edwards, who taught me to be the teacher I am, and Stuart Horwitz, Mike Larsen, Julie Portelance, and all early readers for essential feedback and testimonials. Thank you, Kate Hanley, for the beautiful foreword.

Thank you for your generous endorsements SARK, Tama Kieves, Padma Venkatramen, Robin Kall, Dr. Eric Maisel, Dr. Adam Zwig, Renee Baribeau, Julie Gerstenblatt, Dr. Craig Malkin, Carla Naumburg, Lynne Heinzmann, Jacquelyn Mitchard, and Dr. Patricia Muehsam.

To my literary community and colleagues, in addition to those just mentioned for endorsements: Willett Free poetry group and librarians headed by Jennifer Shaker, Tracy Hart, Sam Bennett, Octavia

Randolph, Janice Harper, Stuart Horwitz, Simon Golden, Stephanie Chandler, Carla King, and the Nonfiction Writers Conference; The Virginia Festival of the Book; Sean Murphy and 1455 Summer Festival; Best Ever You's Elizabeth Guarino; local bookstores, Curiosity & Co., Wakefield Books, Books on the Square; and so many more—you know who you are—thank you! To the communities at Omega Institute and Kripalu—namaste. How I struggled with my book description—thank you Kevin Grant; Luke, Will, and Tom Patterson; Kia and Sophia Kofoed, Paula Schonewald, Tama Kieves and Melissa Sones.

To Harvard Medical School publishing course colleagues, in appreciation for the dozen years we shared helping medical professionals reach the public with their knowledge and wisdom, especially Julie Silver, MD.

Thank you to my supportive and loving family including the Tener, Yudkowsky and Arnold, Yomtov, Herschlag, Patterson, Potter, Sammis, and Cabot clans.

To our beloved Labradoodle Sophie—I miss you every day. You were a part of this journey, completed our family, and gave us unconditional love. I wish I took you up more often on your invitations to leave the computer and romp and wag my tail!

It would take a whole book to properly thank every teacher, client, class participant, colleague, friend, and family member who has inspired, taught, and supported me—and in some way impacted the book in your hands. Please know how grateful I am for your loving and generous presence in my life. I have worked on *Breathe. Write. Breathe.* for many years and in that time, memory fades. I fear I've left out someone instrumental in the early stages. Please accept my appreciation and plea for forgiveness for any omissions.

Breathe. Write. Breathe. is dedicated to my family:

In memory of Mimi—a creative spirit, a bright light, a supportive and loving presence—and of my bibliophilic parents, Marty and Elizabeth, who encouraged my writing from an early age and were role models for an artistic and literary life.

Dedicated with love to my three men—Tom, Will, and Luke. How did I get so lucky?

RECOMMENDED RESOURCES FOR YOU

Many beloved teachers, books, and workshops inspired my work with writing, breath work, movement, and personal/spiritual growth. Here are some of my favorite resources. I encourage you to explore any that intrigue you.

WEBSITES AND VIDEOS

Qigong

- Robert Peng's website: RobertPeng.com
  YouTube channel: Robert Peng
- Leah Franklin's website: QiMastersClass.com
  YouTube channel: Qi Masters Class
- Lee Holden's website: HoldenQiGong.com
  YouTube channel: Holden QiGong
- Daisy Lee's website: RadiantLotusQigong.com
  YouTube channel: Daisy Lee

Yoga, Meditation, and Other Practices

- YogaJournal.com
- Meditation teacher and author Will Johnson's website: embodiment.net
- Kari Hohne's CafeAuSoul.com for an excellent dream dictionary, I Ching reading, and other delights for the soul

BOOKS

- Chitty, John and Mary Louise Muller. *Energy Exercises: Easy Exercises for Health and Vitality.* Silver Lake, Wisconsin: New Leaf Distributing Company, 1990, 2018.
- Johnson, Will. Any of his books on meditation and spiritual practices.

- Maisel, Eric. Anything by this creativity coach! Two of his books I've contributed to are: *The Creativity Workbook for Coaches and Creatives: 50+ Inspiring Exercises from Creativity Coaches Worldwide.* New York: Routledge, 2020. And *The Coach's Guide to Completing Creative Work.* New York: Routledge, 2023.
- Muehsam, Patricia, *Beyond Medicine: A Physician's Revolutionary Prescription for Achieving Absolute Health and Finding Inner Peace.* Novato, California: New World Library
- Peng, Robert. *The Master Key: Qigong Secrets for Vitality, Love, and Wisdom.* Boulder, CO: Sounds True, Inc., 2014.

ADDITIONAL DETAILS AND QUOTATIONS FROM THE CREATIVITY AND RELAXATION RESEARCH REFERRED TO IN CHAPTERS 1 AND 2:

"Exploring the impact of acute physical activity on creative thinking: a comprehensive narrative review with a focus on activity type and intensity," published in *Discover Psychology,* states, "One key finding is the enhancement of divergent thinking, a critical component of creativity, through activities like walking at a natural pace. Moderate intensity aerobic exercise and dance, though based on limited studies, also appear to facilitate divergent thinking. Additionally, vigorous intensity aerobic exercise may enhance secondary aspects of divergent thinking, including the quantity and flexibility of idea generation."

Additionally, a research study from Middlesex University in the UK titled "Exercise Enhances Creativity Independently of Mood," published in the *British Journal of Sports Medicine,* found that exercise helps people be more creative. They didn't study qigong bouncing specifically (surprise?), but surely bouncing can be considered exercise.

In an article in *Inc.*, Geoffrey James writes, "Scientists studying brain scans recently discovered that moments of creativity take place when the mind is at rest rather than working on something."

In *Beyond Medicine*, Patricia Muehsam, MD, writes, "By gentle, slow breathing—and specifically, belly or abdominal breathing—we can instantaneously turn on our parasympathetic nervous system, enabling rest, repair, rejuvenation, healing, digestion, and sleep." When I emailed her asking her to tie the science to creativity, she wrote, "This state of parasympathetic nervous system activation calms the mind and relaxes the body. That's where we need to be to 'flow,' to get our creative juices flowing. We can't access our inner muse otherwise." She also points out: "When the sympathetic nervous system is activated, that state will completely inhibit/stifle/thwart our creative process."

"A 2020 thematic literature review on Mindfulness and Creativity" by Danah Henriksen, Carmen Richardson, and Kyle Shack concludes that, "Mindfulness practices improve skills or habits of mind that can support creativity." Dr. Jon Kabat-Zinn defines mindfulness as a state of "nonjudgmental, moment-to-moment awareness."

STUDIES AND ARTICLES

- Chen, Chong. "Exploring the impact of acute physical activity on creative thinking: a comprehensive narrative review with a focus on activity type and intensity." *Discover Psychology*, (2024) 4:3. https://doi.org/10.1007/s44202-024-00114-9A.
- Henriksen, Danah, Carmen Richardson, and Kyle Shack. "A 2020 thematic literature review on Mindfulness and Creativity." *Thinking Skills and Creativity Journal*, (September 2023)
- Henriksen, Danah, Carmen Richardson, and Kyle Shack. "Mindfulness and creativity: Implications for thinking and learning." *Elsevier, August 1, 2020. https://w*ww.ncbi.nlm.nih.gov/pmc/articles/PMC7395604/
- James, Geoffrey. "Neuroscience: Relaxing Makes You More Creative," Inc.com. Jan 12, 2015. https://www.inc.com/geoffrey james/neuroscience-relaxing-makes-you-more-creative.html

- Kounios , John and Mark Beeman. "The Aha! Moment: the Neural Basis of Solving Problems with Insight." CreativityPost.com, November 11, 2011. http://www.creativitypost.com/science/the_aha_moment._the_cognitive_neuroscience_of_insight

GLOSSARY

Chakras: Sanskrit term for energy centers in the body, literally, "spinning wheels." The seven major chakras occur along the midline of the body from the root at the perineum to the crown chakra at the top of the skull.

Dantian or dan tian: In Traditional Chinese Medicine or Chinese martial arts, dantian refers to one of three centers where energy is stored and cultivated in the body. Translated as "elixir field" or "sea of qi," the three dantians are often referred to as the "three treasures."

Upper Dantian: The energy center in the head, considered the wisdom center of the body.

Middle Dantian: The energy center around the heart, considered the love center.

Lower Dantian: The vitality center of the body, located three fingers' width below the navel and centered in the abdominal cavity.

Elements: Many metaphysical systems incorporate the elements to describe various types of energy and how they relate to the energy centers of the body (chakras, dantians, etc.). In yoga, the elements are earth, air, fire, water, and ether. In Taoist cosmology, the elements are wood, fire, earth, metal, and water.

Kabbalah: A mystical path in Judaism that focuses on experiencing the hidden reality of Creation.

Meridian: Energy pathways in the body (Traditional Chinese Medicine)

Ming Men: The energy point (and acupressure point) located between the kidneys. Often referred to as the "Gate of Life" or "Door of Life" (as when we practice "Knocking on the Door of Life").

Neigong: A subset of qigong and an internal martial art rooted in Taoism that employs breathing, movement, postures, and visualization. The practices tonify the soft tissues of the body—muscles, fascia, ligaments, and tendons—and have been documented to provide numerous health benefits.

Pranayama: According to the Oxford Dictionary, "the regulation of the breath through certain techniques and exercises." The Sanskrit word comes from "prana" or "breath" and "ayama" or "restraint."

Qi: Chinese word for the vital life force energy, similar to "prana" in Sanskrit.

Qigong: Stems from meditation, ancient Chinese philosophy, Traditional Chinese Medicine, and Chinese martial arts. Qigong practices involve breathing, movement, and meditation.

Sufism: A mystical practice within Islam. Sufi is a practitioner of Sufism.

Yoga: Centuries-old practices that involve breathing techniques, meditation, and physical postures. The eight limbs of yoga include additional aspects, including devotion, service, wisdom, and ritual. Most yogic practices originated in India; over the years, many schools of yoga have proliferated, with various intentions, foundations, and foci.

ABOUT THE AUTHOR

Lisa Tener helps you bring your authentic voice and wisdom to the page. Her book *The Joy of Writing Journal* won five book awards. For her work as a book coach, Lisa was awarded Mentor/Coach of the Year by the Stevie Awards for Women in Business. Lisa served on the faculty of Harvard Medical School's continuing medical education publishing course for over a dozen years. Lisa holds bachelor's and master's degrees from MIT and is certified by RP Qigong to teach Empowerments and Happiness Qigong. Lisa lives with her husband and teenage son in Rhode Island.

Connect with Lisa:
LisaTener.com
X: @LisaTener
Instagram: @lisa_tener_writes
Facebook: WriteandCreatewithLisaTener
#BreatheWriteBreathe

Check out Lisa's book writing programs, book proposal support, editor referral service, articles, free writing and publishing resources, and more at LisaTener.com

Made in the USA
Las Vegas, NV
27 December 2024